Classroom Clips

CURRICULUM COPY ART

by Marilynn G. Barr

Publisher: Roberta Suid
Editor: Carol Whiteley

ISBN 1-878279-21-1

For information about our audio products, write us at:
Newbridge Book Clubs, 3000 Cindel Drive, Delran NJ 08370

Printed in the United States of America
9 8 7 6 5 4 3 2 1

Table of Contents

INTRODUCTION

How to Use the
Card Sets and Patterns

Cards Sets

• As Flashcards

These card sets are excellent for individual skills practice. As a variation white out the information on the cards to create new flashcards for multiplication practice, spelling words, matching, and sequencing activities.

• As Game Cards

Children will enjoy playing Memory with duplicate card sets. Create a trivia game for your class. Reproduce card sets and a second set of cards with questions pertaining to the specific subject areas. Example: Reproduce the invention facts cards, one set with invention facts, one set with questions. Then color and laminate them.

• For Matching and Sorting Activities

The Animal Babies and Animal Tracks are perfect for a memory/matching activity. With cards face down, children play, in turn, the same way they would play the popular Memory game. The child with the most cards wins.

• To Decorate Subject File Folders

Both card set art and clips collection art are great file folder decorations. Children will enjoy decorating book report covers, as well as theme project posters.

The United States, Canada, and the Continents

These card sets and patterns are suitable for memory card games, alphabetizing, and same/different sorting activities. The outline maps are great for book report covers as well as pinpointing geographical locations on each.

Dominos

These giant dominos are ideal for matching activities. Reproduce each and provide each child with his own set. You can begin play at the beginning of a specific time period and allow children to match their domino to one previously played as a bonus activity - a great motivational tool. Score the points as you would in an actual game of dominos.

Clips Collections

Here is a wonderful reference library of illustrations you can duplicate or enlarge for classroom displays, decorative art on worksheets, and to turn into gifts.

Craft and Gift Ideas

This section provides you with directions and diagrams for five different projects:

Greeting Cards

The children can decorate handmade construction paper cards for virtually any occasion with the clips collections and card set art.

Picture Frames

Customizing picture frames for gifts is easy. Sportsmen and women will enjoy customized baseball and/or tennis decorated frames made from construction paper and paper plates. Cut out the center of the paper plate and mount the bottom of the plate on a round or square sheet of construction paper

Doorknob Hangers

Here also customizing doorknob hangers for personal use or as gift items is fun. For a computer whiz use the computer art on the Classroom Symbols-Clips Collection page.

Refrigerator Magnets

The cards set art characters are great for refrigerator magnets with space for a message (eliminate the words first) and magnetic tape. Children can mount the patterns on construction paper or laminate them and mount the magnetic tape directly on the back. (For durability, have children mount the magnetic tape prior to laminating.)

Bookmarks

Children can glue art from the card sets and/or Clips Collections to one end of a 1" x 6" strip of colored construction paper, then laminate.

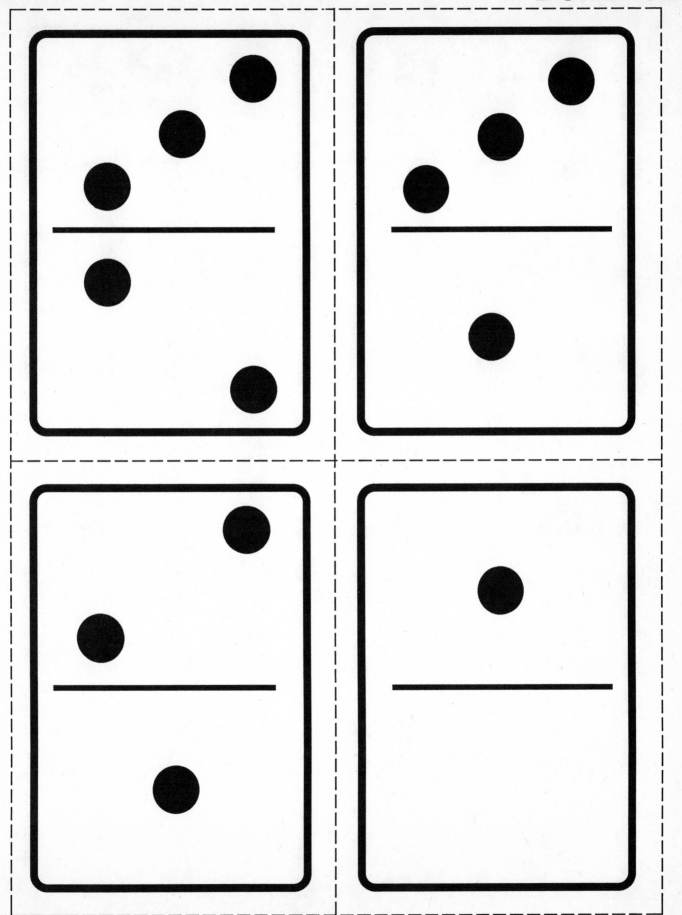

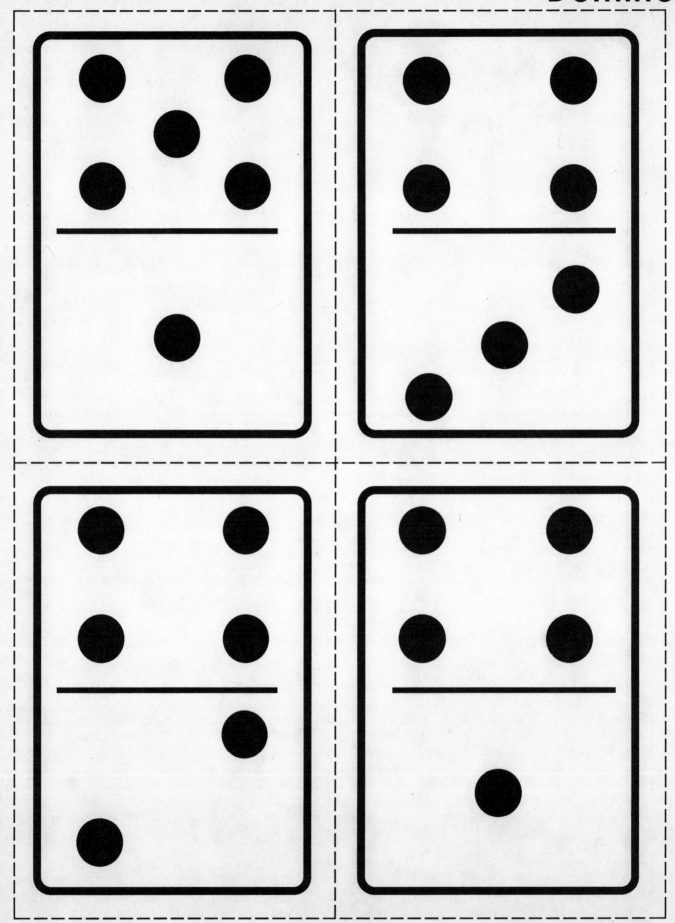

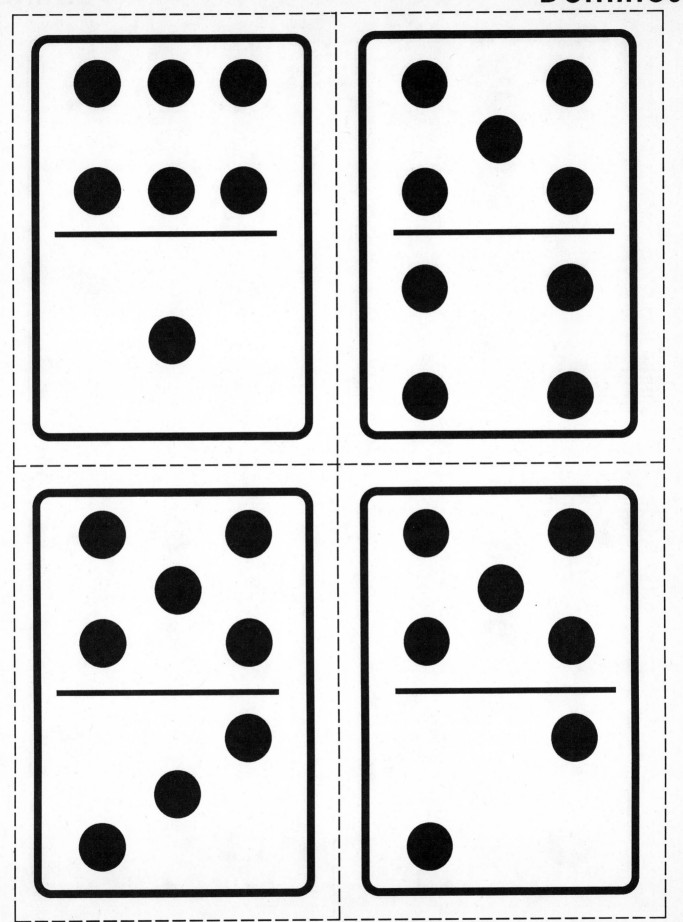

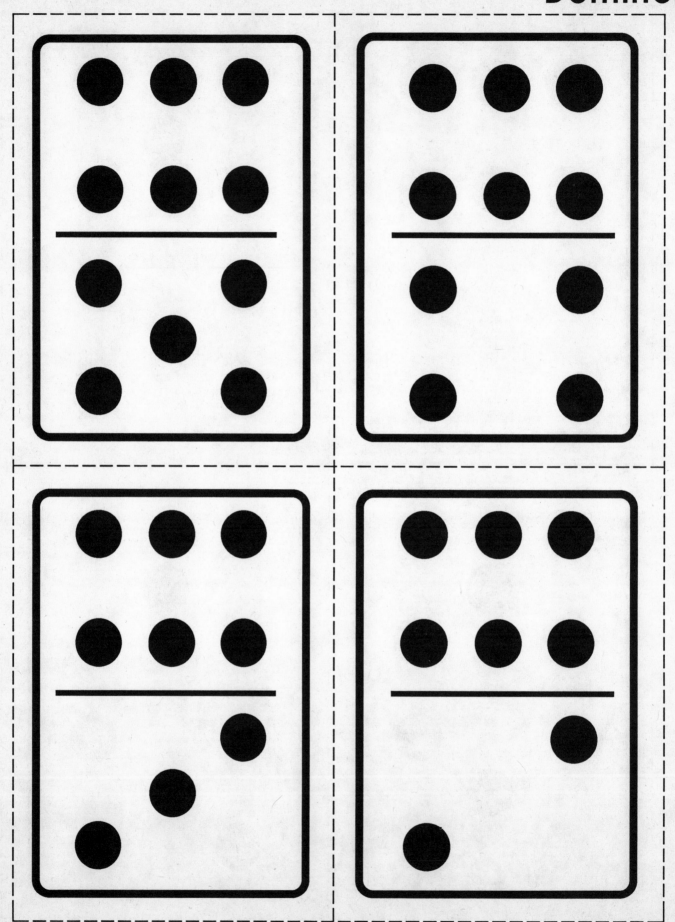

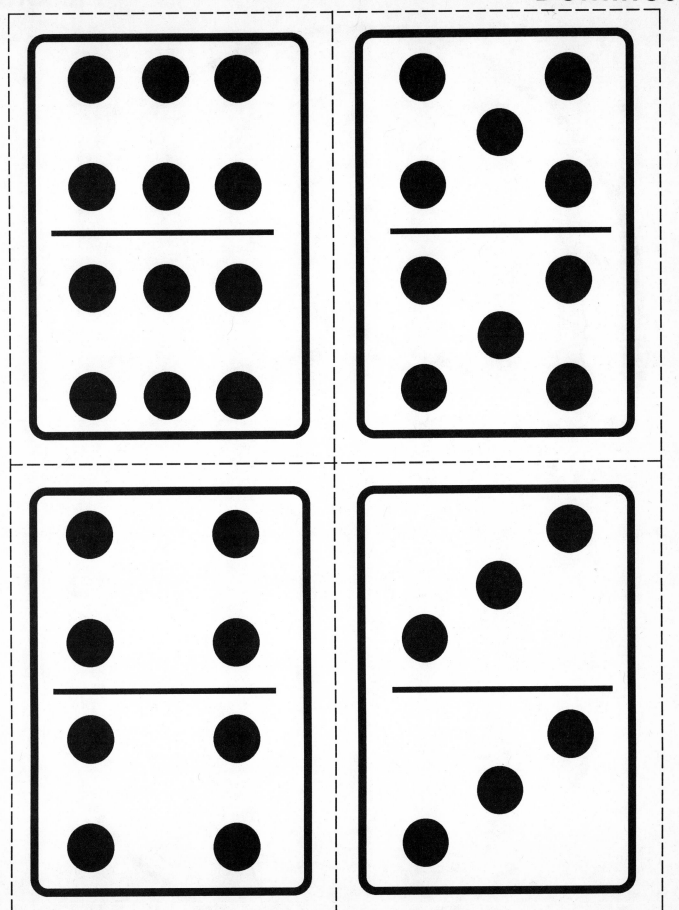

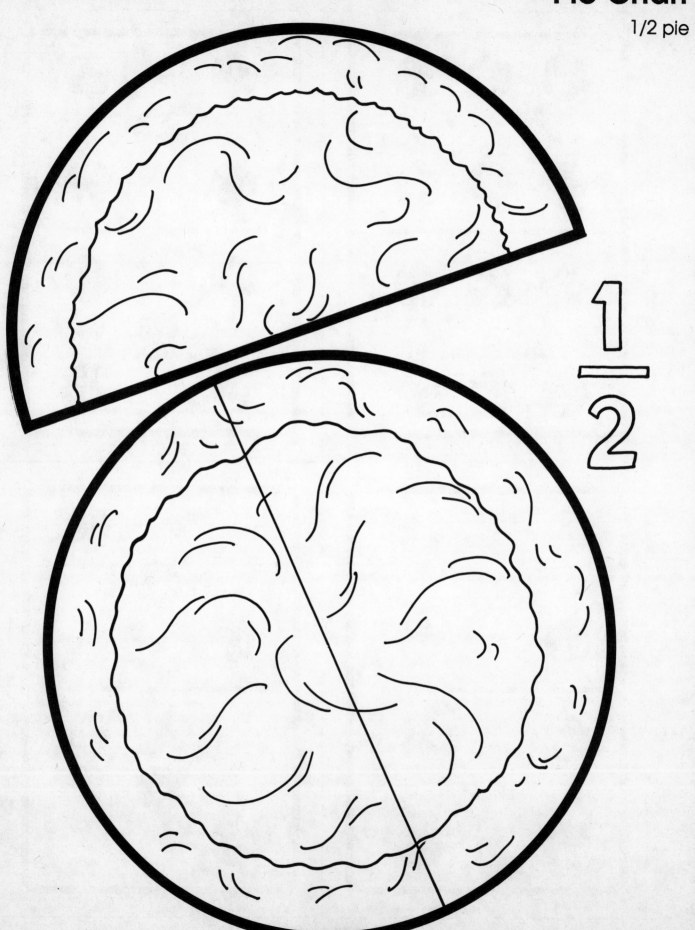

$\dfrac{1}{2}$

$\dfrac{1}{3}$

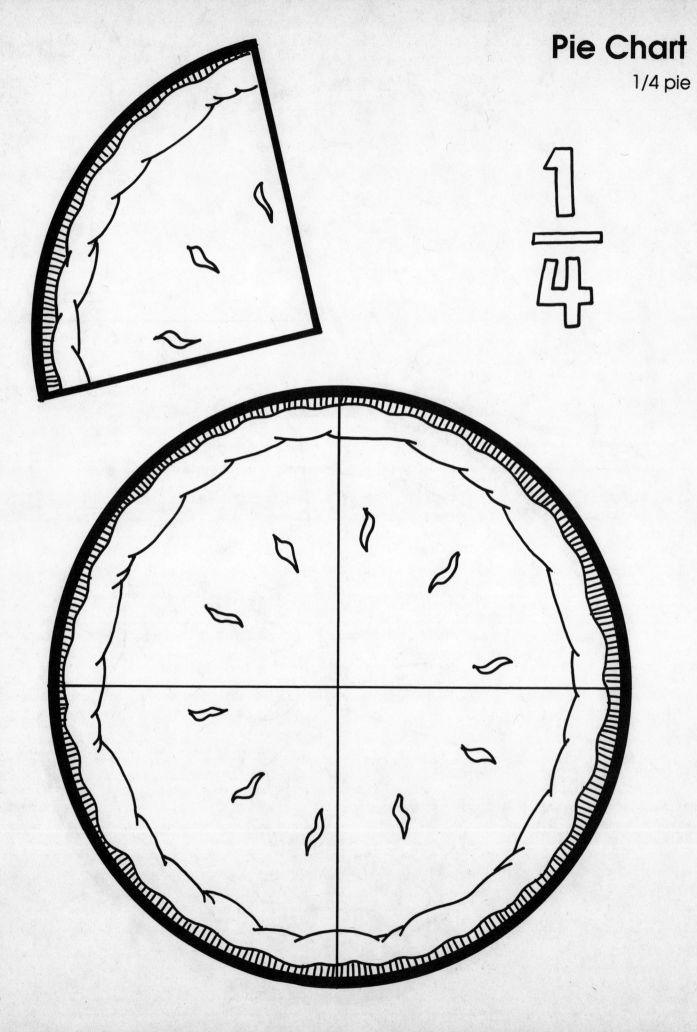

$\frac{1}{4}$

$$\frac{1}{8}$$

Sundial

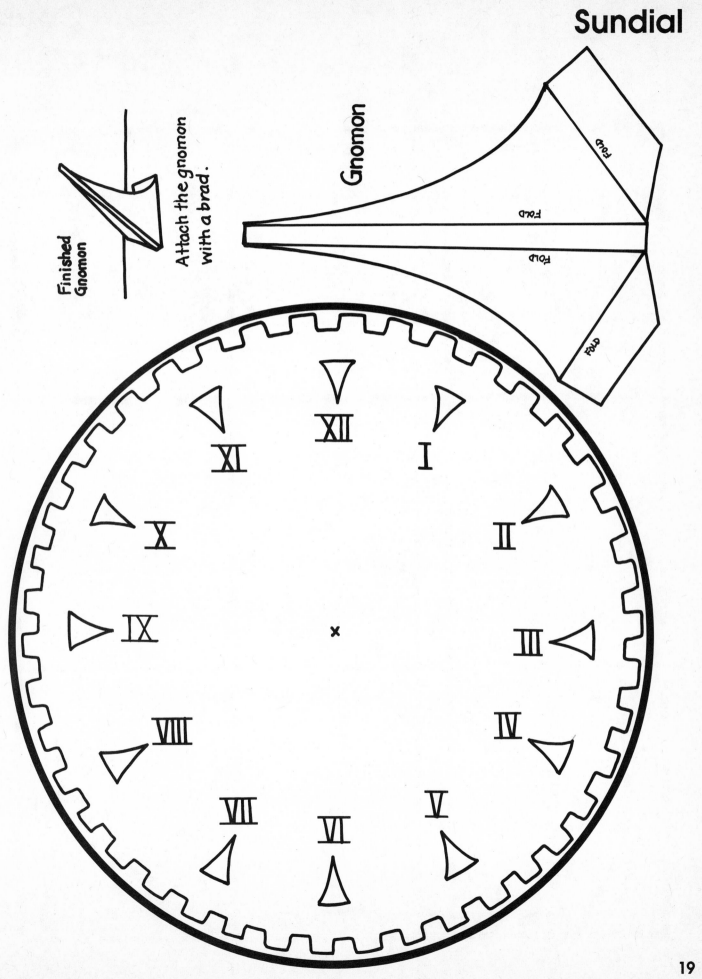

Gnomon

Finished Gnomon

Attach the gnomon with a brad.

FOLD

FOLD

FOLD

FOLD

XII

XI

I

X

II

IX

III

VIII

IV

VII

VI

V

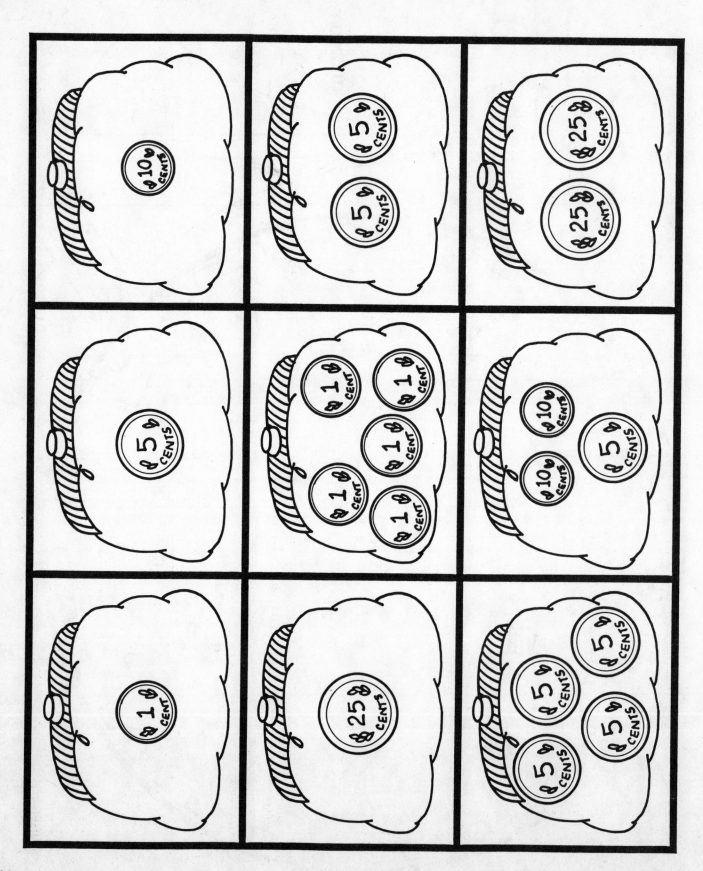

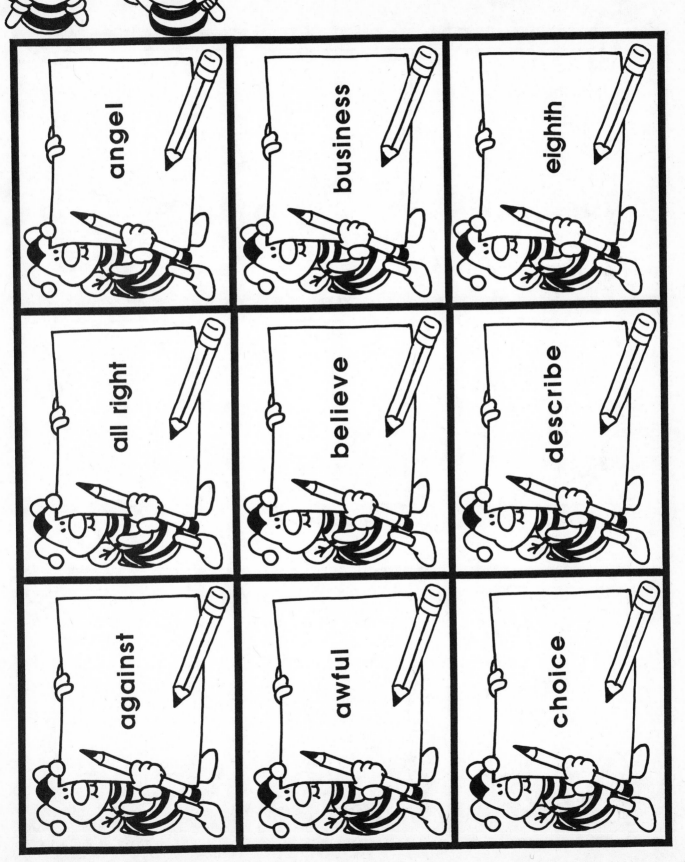

angel

business

eighth

all right

believe

describe

against

awful

choice

Commonly Misspelled Words

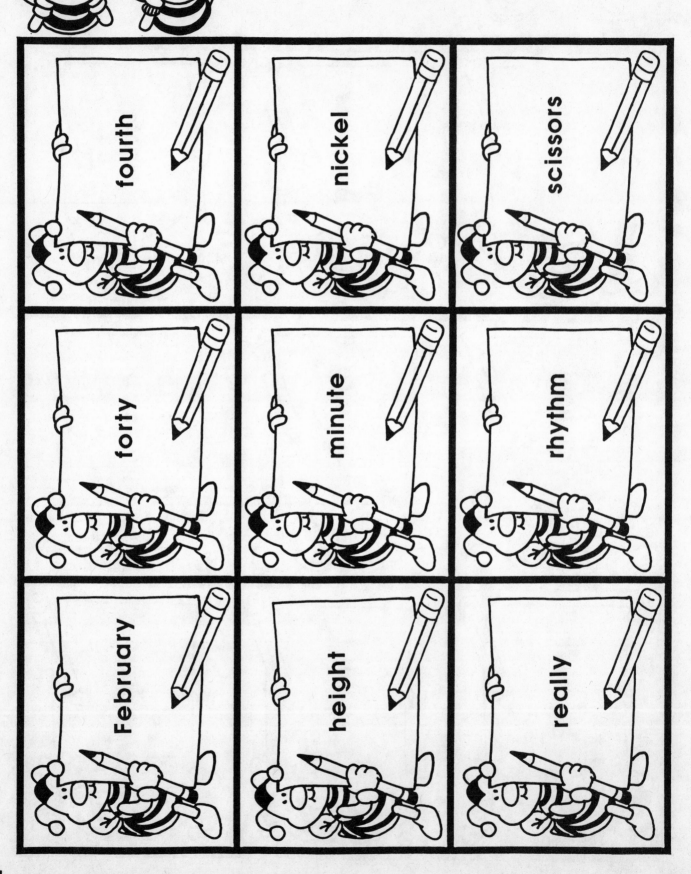

fourth

nickel

scissors

forty

minute

rhythm

February

height

really

Editing Symbols

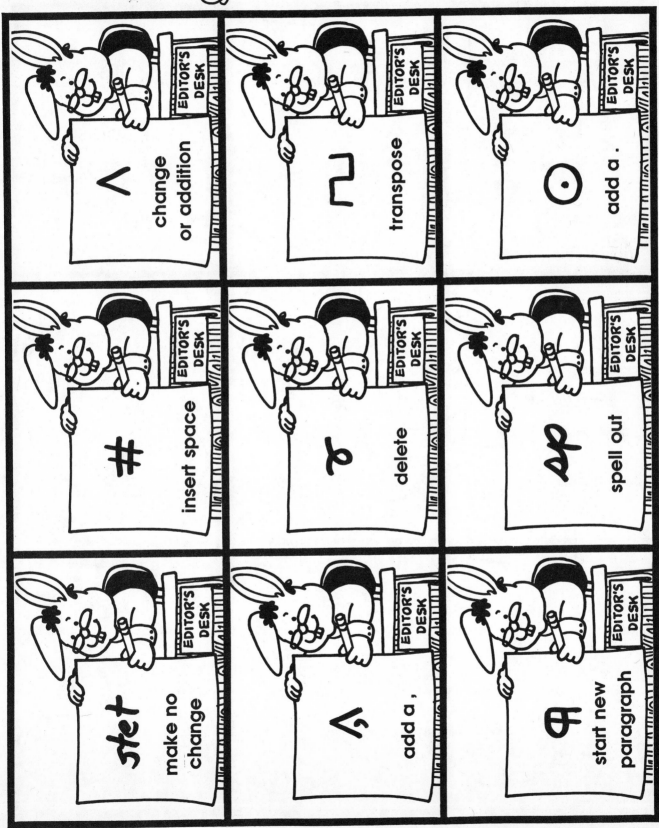

∧ change or addition	⊃ transpose	⊙ add a .
# insert space	ℓ delete	sp spell out
stet make no change	∧ add a ,	¶ start new paragraph

Capitalize names of countries, states, and cities.

Capitalize names of rivers, oceans, islands, and mountains.

Capitalize names of ships, trains, planes, submarines, and satellites.

Capitalize days of the week, months, and holidays.

Capitalize names of streets, highways, plazas, parks, squares, and buildings.

Capitalize names of historical events, wars, treaties, laws, and documents.

Capitalize proper nouns.

Capitalize names of nationalities and tribes.

Capitalize names of stars, planets, and constellations.

!	;	?
single quotation mark	semicolon	question mark
!	,	.
exclamation point	comma	period
:	( )	''
colon	parenthesis	quotation marks

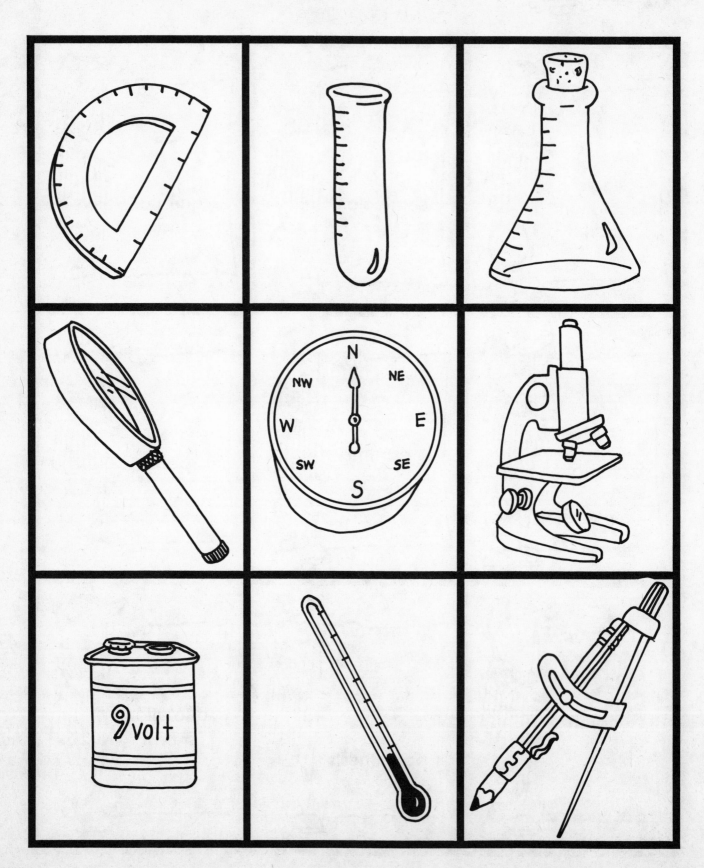

Clips Collection
Inventions

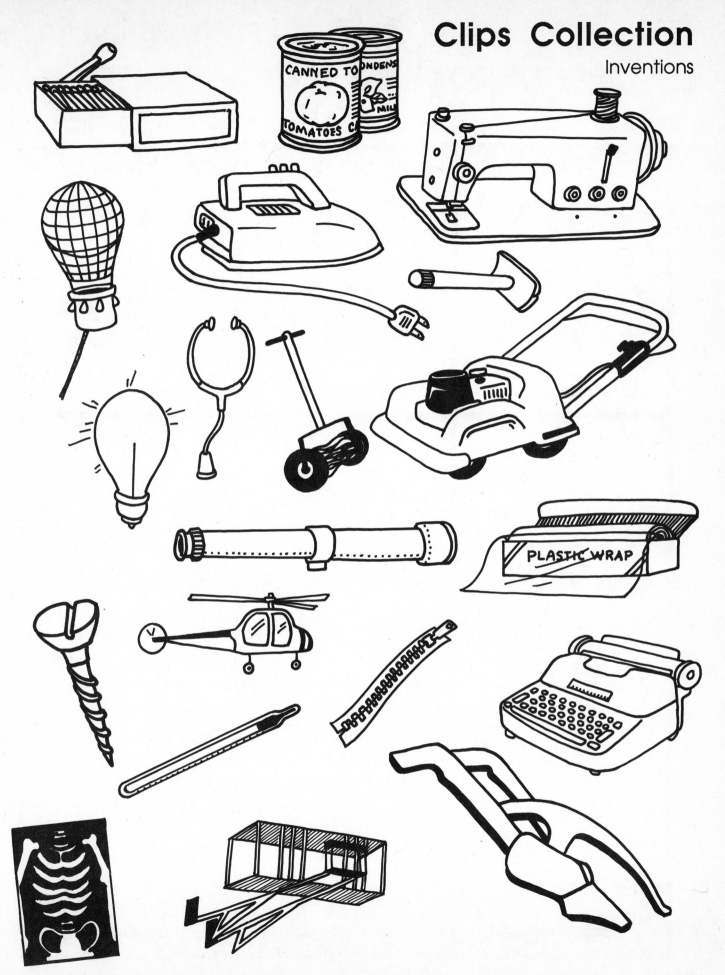

PLASTIC WRAP

CANNED TOMATOES

TOMATOES

29

Incandescent Light
Thomas A. Edison
(United States)
1879

Sewing Machine
Elias Howe
(United States)
1845

Zipper
Whitcomb L. Judson
(United States)
1892

Stethoscope
Rene T. H. Laennec
(France)
1816

Thermometer
Galileo
(Italy)
1593

Electric Iron
Henry W. Seely
(United States)
1882

Safety Matches
Gustave E. Pasch
(Sweden)
1844

Safety Razor
King C. Gillette
(United States)
1895

X-ray
Wilhelm K. Roentgen
(Germany)
1895

Telescope
Hans Lippershey
(Netherlands)
1608

Typewriter Christopher Sholes
(United States)
1867

Balloon
Jacques and
Joseph Montgolfier
(France)
1783

Plow
Egypt &
Mesopotamia
c. 3000's B.C.

Cellophane
Jacques
Brandenberger
(Switzerland)
1908

Canned Foods
Nicolas Appert
(France)
1787-1810

Helicopter
Louis and Jacques
Breguet
(France)
1907

Airplane
Orville & Wilbur
Wright
(United States)
1903

Screw
Archimedes
(Greece)
200's B.C.

Weights and Measures

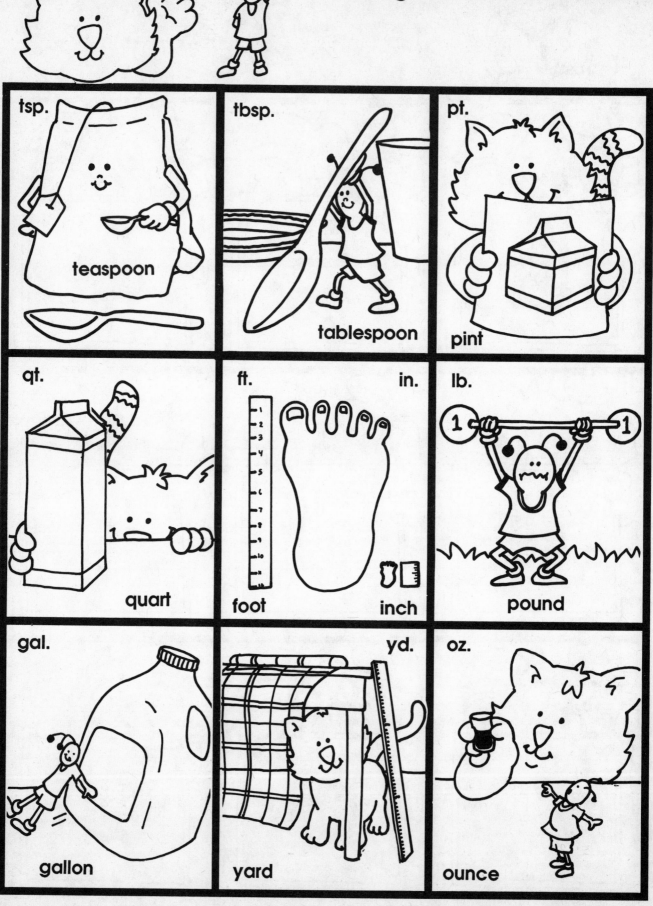

tsp.	tbsp.	pt.
teaspoon	tablespoon	pint

qt.	ft. in.	lb.
quart	foot inch	pound

gal.	yd.	oz.
gallon	yard	ounce

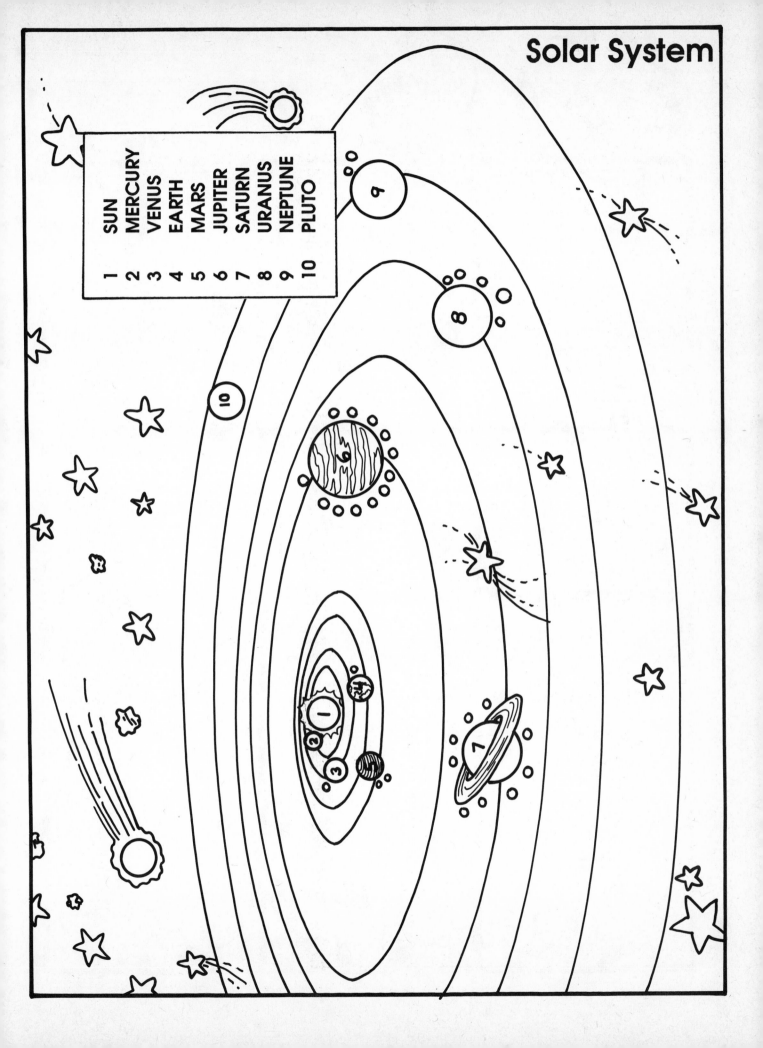

Earth
Third planet from the sun
Diameter: approx. 7,900 miles
1 moon

Saturn
Sixth planet from the sun
Diameter: approx. 71,500 miles
9 moons

Pluto
Ninth planet from the sun
Diameter: approx. 3,500 miles

Venus
Second planet from the sun
Diameter: approx. 7,700 miles

Jupiter
Fifth planet from the sun
Diameter: approx. 88,000 miles
12 moons

Neptune
Eighth planet from the sun
Diameter: approx. 30,000 miles
2 moons

Mercury
First planet from the sun
Diameter: approx. 3,100 miles

Mars
Fourth planet from the sun
Diameter: approx. 4,200 miles
2 moons

Uranus
Seventh planet from the sun
Diameter: approx. 28,500 miles
5 moons

Plant Poster

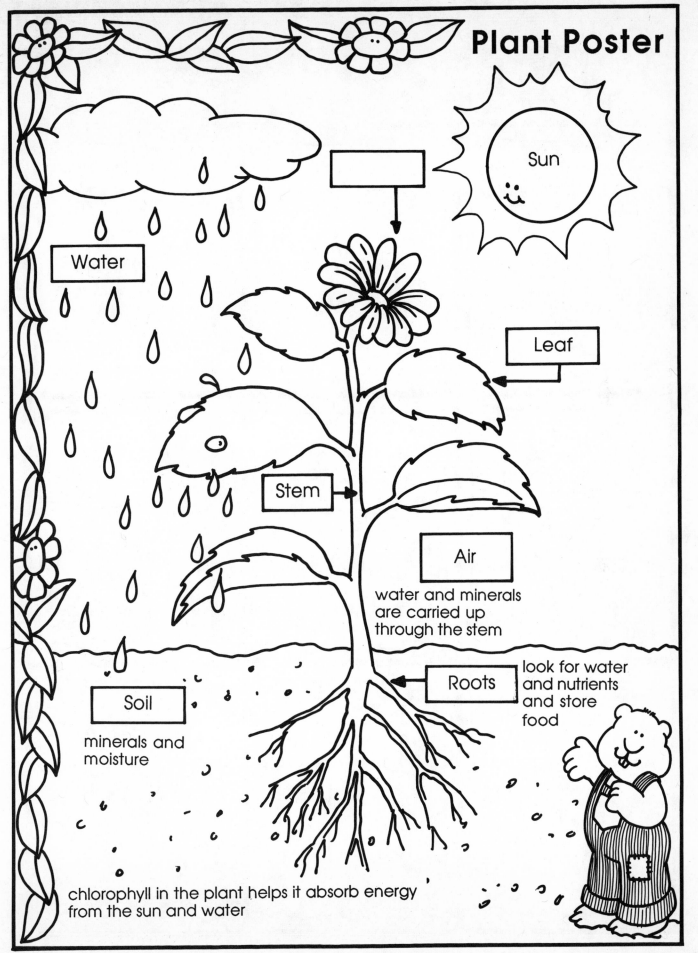

Sun

Water

Leaf

Stem

Air

water and minerals
are carried up
through the stem

Roots

look for water
and nutrients
and store
food

Soil

minerals and
moisture

chlorophyll in the plant helps it absorb energy
from the sun and water

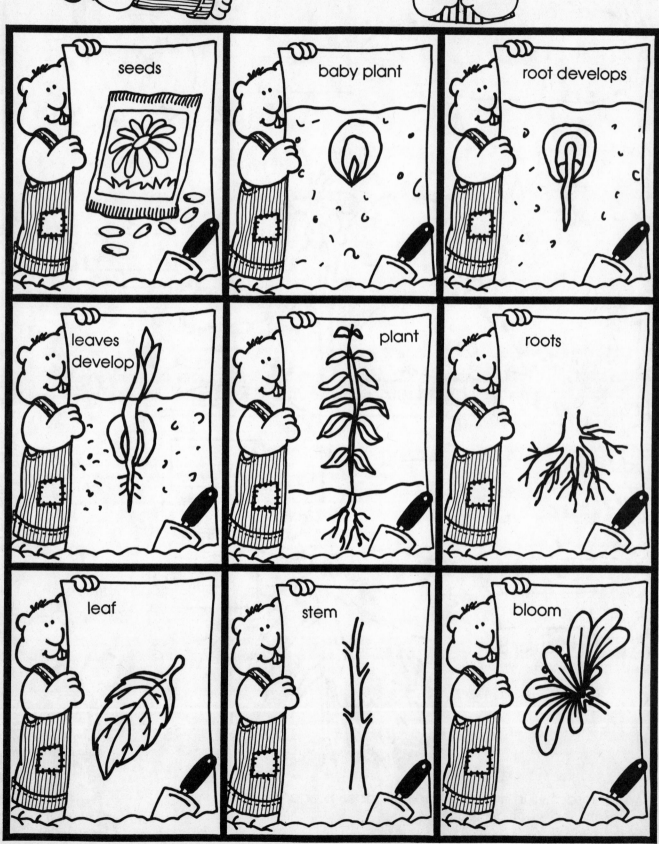

seeds	baby plant	root develops
leaves develop	plant	roots
leaf	stem	bloom

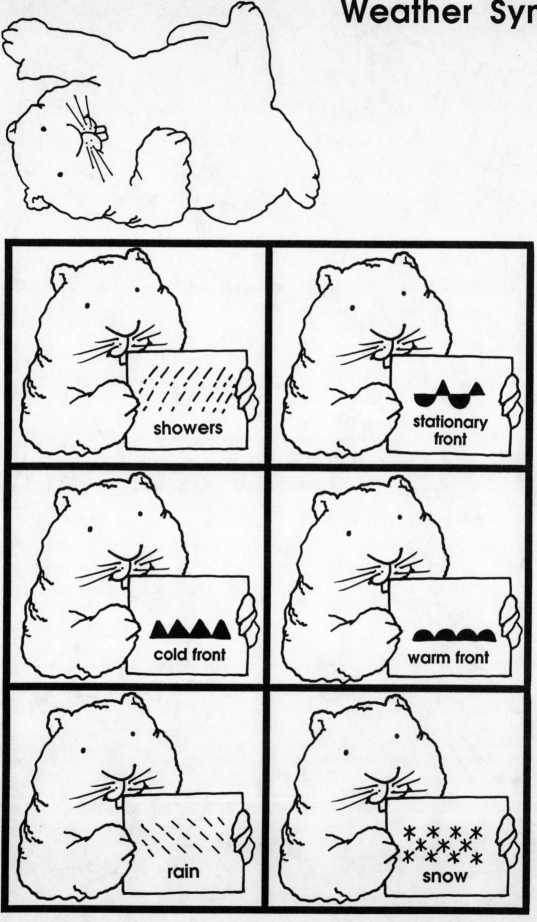

showers

stationary front

cold front

warm front

rain

snow

partly
cloudy

clear

cloudy

hurricane

9
tropical
storm

thunder
storms

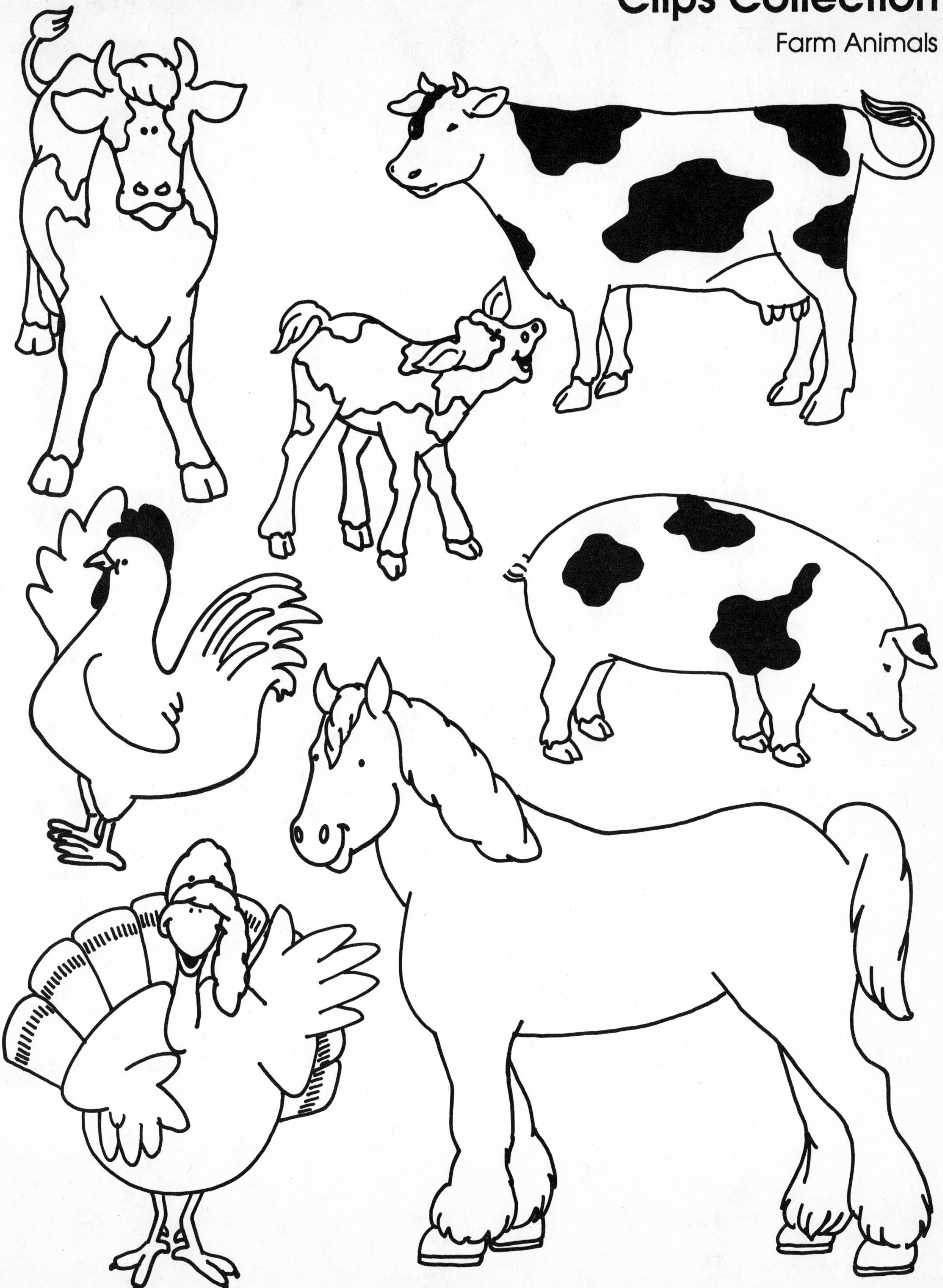

Clips Collection

Animals

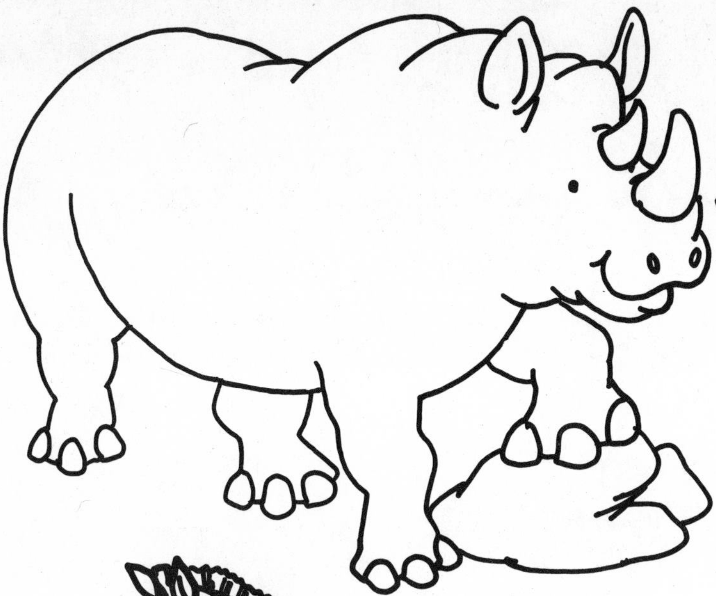

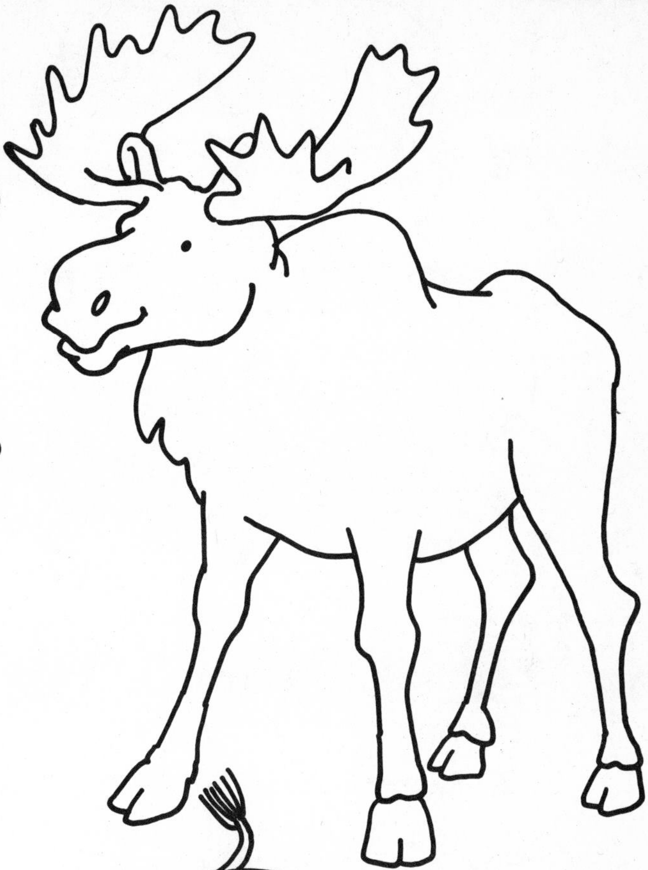

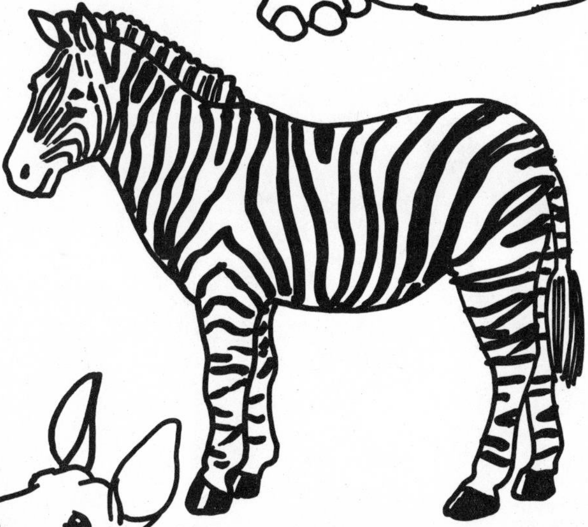

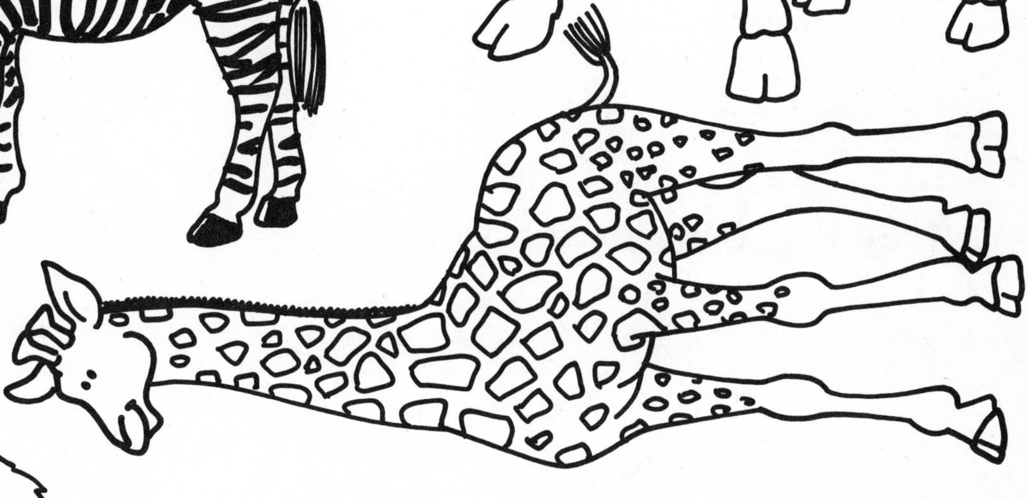

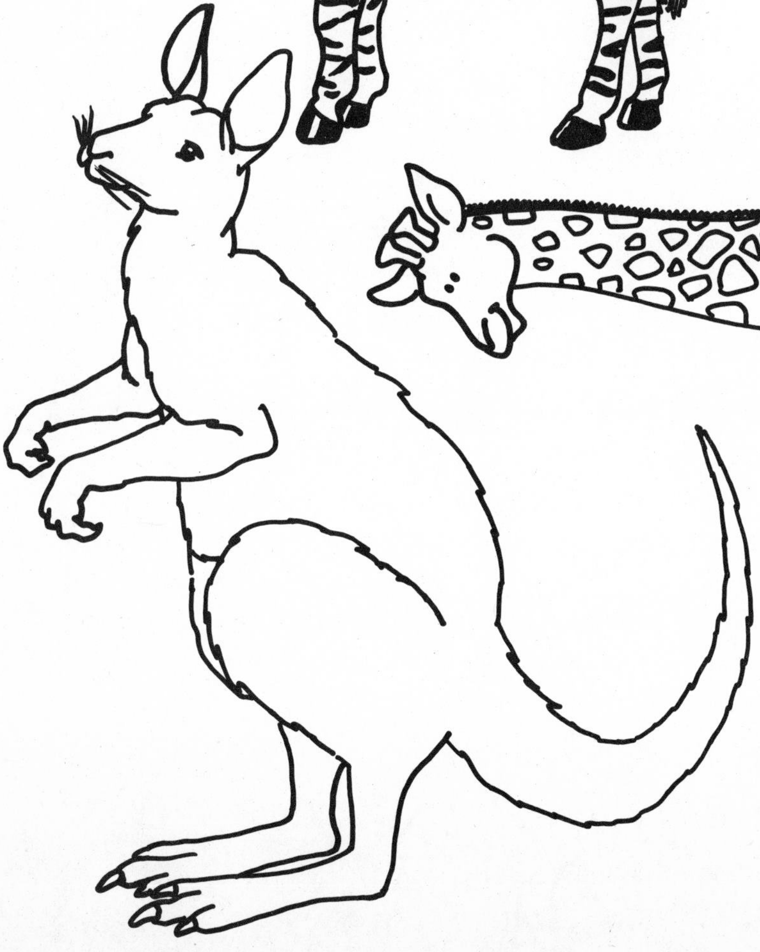

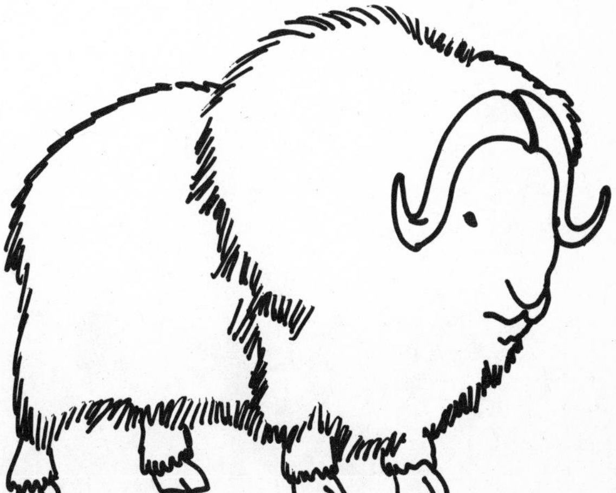

At The Zoo...

NATURAL HABITAT

Wild Kingdom

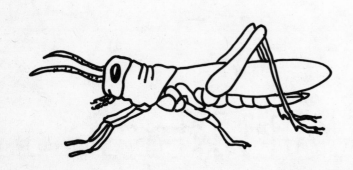

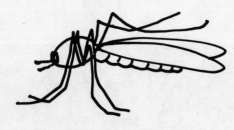

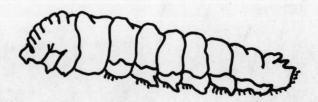

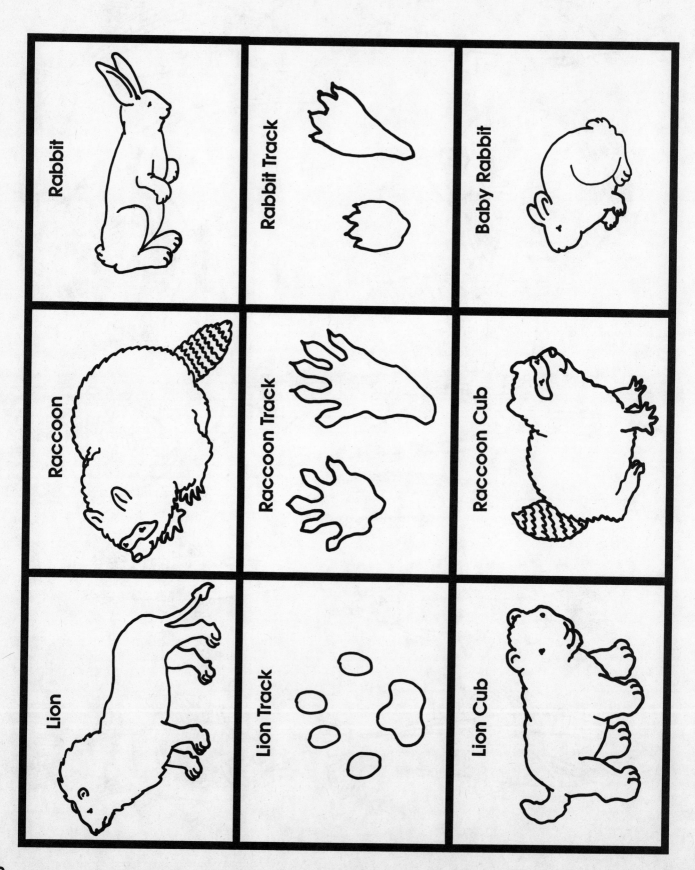

Animal Babies and Animal Tracks

Horse

Horse Track

Foal

Deer

Deer Track

Fawn

Bear

Bear Track

Bear Cub

Ankylosaurus

Brontosaurus

Dimetrodon

Elasmosaurus

Iguanodon

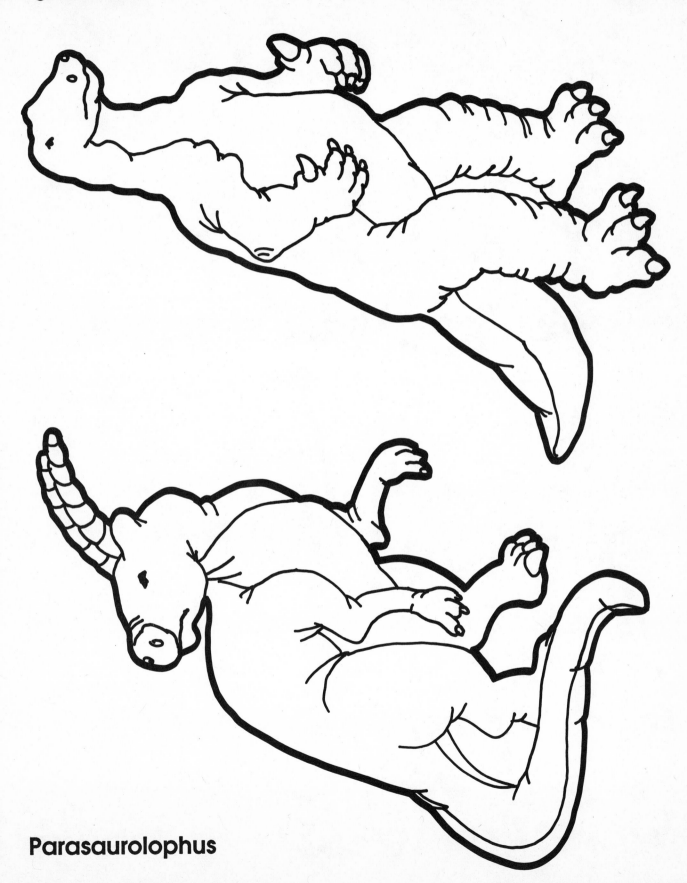

Parasaurolophus

Protoceratops

Pteranodon

56

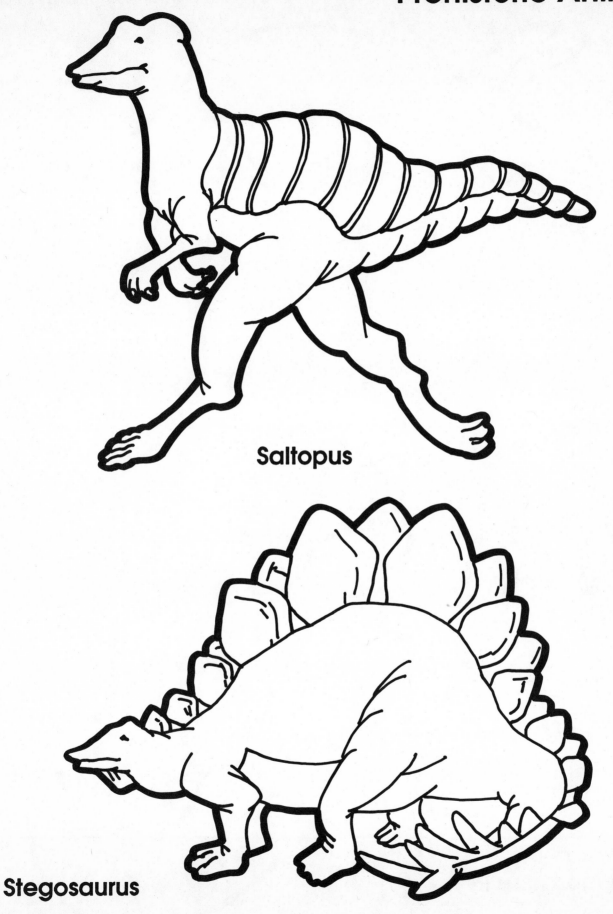

Saltopus

Stegosaurus

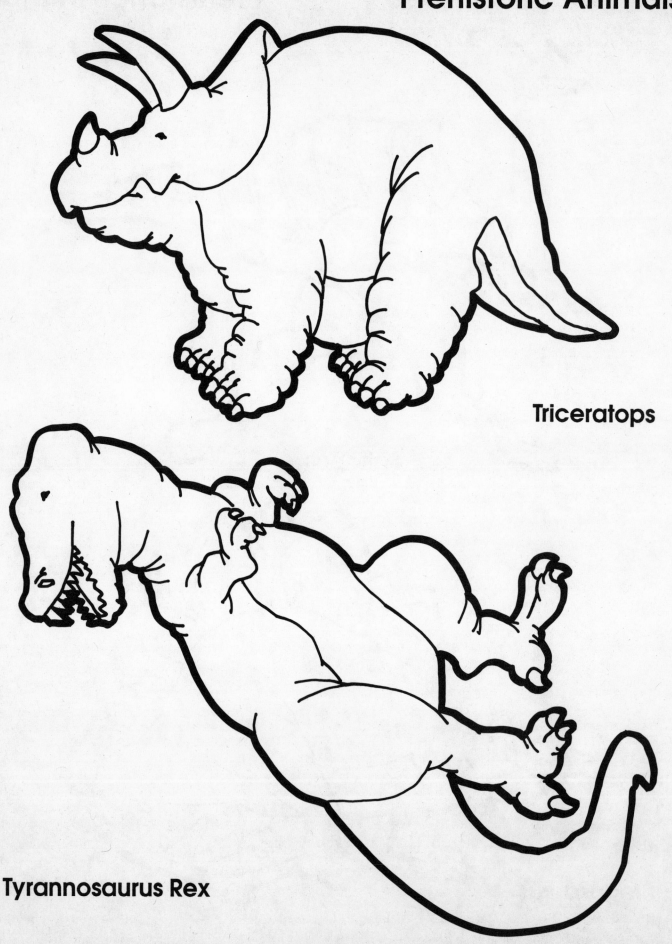

Triceratops

Tyrannosaurus Rex

Prehistoric Animals
Statistics

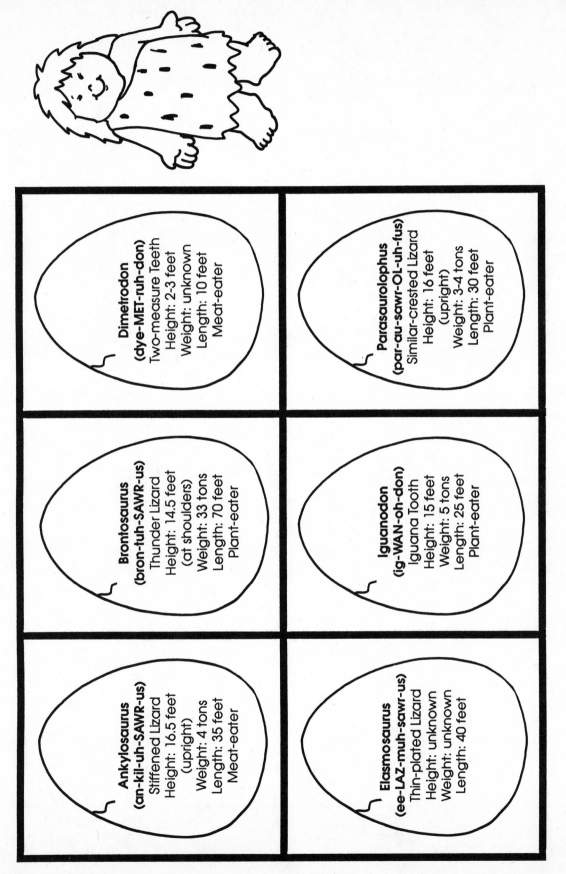

**Dimetrodon
(dye-MET-ruh-don)**
Two-measure Teeth
Height: 2-3 feet
Weight: unknown
Length: 10 feet
Meat-eater

**Parasaurolophus
(par-au-sawr-OL-uh-fus)**
Similar-crested Lizard
Height: 16 feet
(upright)
Weight: 3-4 tons
Length: 30 feet
Plant-eater

**Brontosaurus
(bron-tuh-SAWR-us)**
Thunder Lizard
Height: 14.5 feet
(at shoulders)
Weight: 33 tons
Length: 70 feet
Plant-eater

**Iguanodon
(ig-WAN-oh-don)**
Iguana Tooth
Height: 15 feet
Weight: 5 tons
Length: 25 feet
Plant-eater

**Ankylosaurus
(an-kil-uh-SAWR-us)**
Stiffened Lizard
Height: 16.5 feet
(upright)
Weight: 4 tons
Length: 35 feet
Meat-eater

**Elasmosaurus
(ee-LAZ-muh-sawr-us)**
Thin-plated Lizard
Height: unknown
Weight: unknown
Length: 40 feet

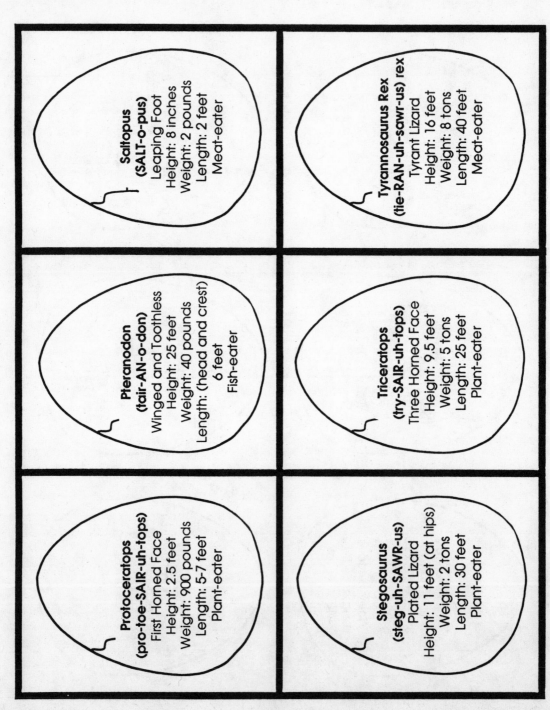

Saltopus
(SALT-o-pus)
Leaping Foot
Height: 8 inches
Weight: 2 pounds
Length: 2 feet
Meat-eater

Tyrannosaurus Rex
(tie-RAN-uh-sawr-us) rex
Tyrant Lizard
Height: 16 feet
Weight: 8 tons
Length: 40 feet
Meat-eater

Pteranodon
(tair-AN-o-don)
Winged and Toothless
Height: 25 feet
Weight: 40 pounds
Length: (head and crest)
6 feet
Fish-eater

Triceratops
(try-SAIR-uh-tops)
Three Horned Face
Height: 9.5 feet
Weight: 5 tons
Length: 25 feet
Plant-eater

Protoceratops
(pro-toe-SAIR-uh-tops)
First Horned Face
Height: 2.5 feet
Weight: 900 pounds
Length: 5-7 feet
Plant-eater

Stegosaurus
(steg-uh-SAWR-us)
Plated Lizard
Height: 11 feet (at hips)
Weight: 2 tons
Length: 30 feet
Plant-eater

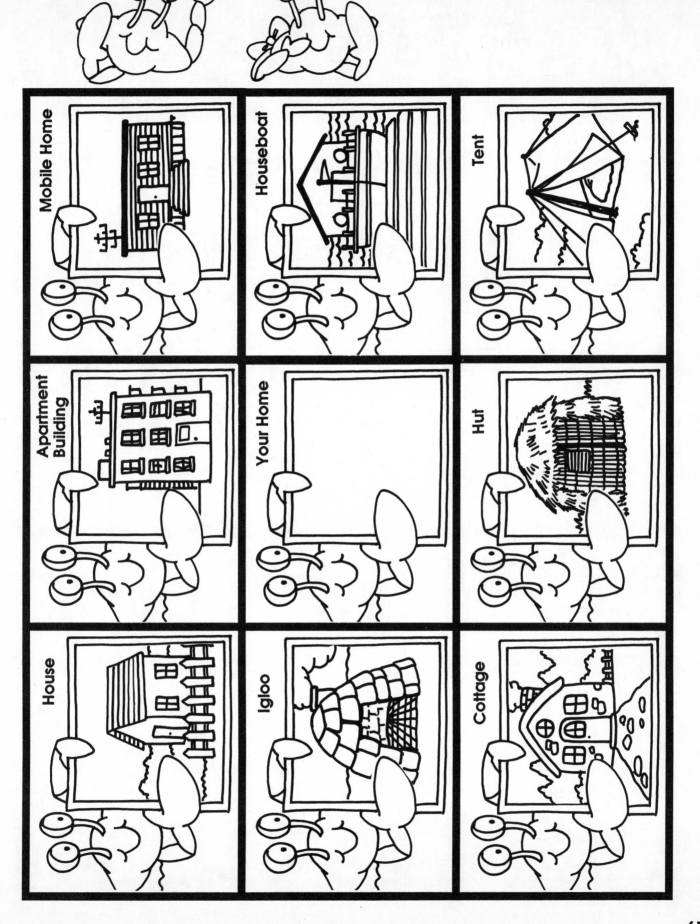

Mobile Home

Houseboat

Tent

Apartment Building

Your Home

Hut

House

Igloo

Cottage

Artist
Leonardo da Vinci

Artist
Walt Disney

Artist
Georgia O'Keeffe

Artist
Vincent van Gogh

Composer
Johann Sebastian Bach

Composer
Ludwig van Beethoven

Writer
Helen Keller

Writer
Charlotte Brontë

Writer
Emily Brontë

Explorer
Samuel de Champlain

Explorer
Christopher Columbus

Explorer
Leif Ericson

Explorer
Matthew Alexander Henson

Explorer
Henry Hudson

Explorer
Lewis Meriwether

Explorer
Ferdinand Magellan

Explorer
Sacagawea

Explorer
Sir Walter Raleigh

Famous People
Leaders

Leader
George Washington

Leader
Gaius Julius Caesar

Leader
Sir Winston Churchill

Leader
Queen Elizabeth I

Leader
Martin Luther King

Leader
Napoleon

Leader
Chief Joseph

Leader
Sun Yat-sen

Leader
Abraham Lincoln

Scientist
Elizabeth Blackwell

Scientist
Louis Braille

Scientist
Marie Sklodowska Curie

Scientist
Thomas Alva Edison

Scientist
Albert Einstein

Scientist
Benjamin Franklin

Scientist
Johannes Gutenberg

Scientist
Sir Issac Newton

Scientist
Jonas Edward Salk

Flower
Camellia

Bird
Yellowhammer

Flower
Forget-Me-Not

Bird
Willow Ptarmigan

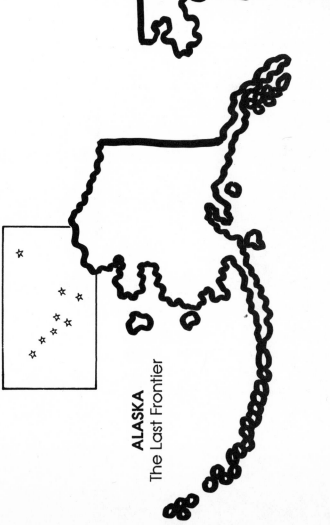

ALABAMA
The Heart of Dixie

ALASKA
The Last Frontier

Flower
Saguaro

Bird
Cactus Wren

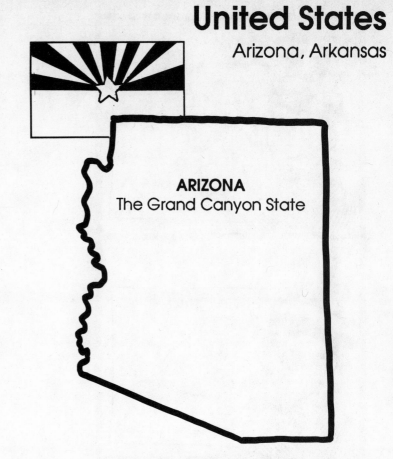

ARIZONA
The Grand Canyon State

Flower
Apple Blossom

Bird
Mockingbird

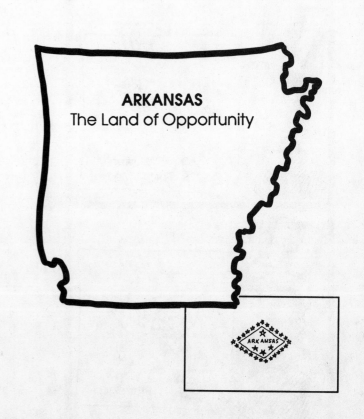

ARKANSAS
The Land of Opportunity

68

Flower
Golden Poppy

Bird
California Valley Quail

CALIFORNIA
The Golden State

CALIFORNIA REPUBLIC

Flower
Rocky Mountain Columbine

Bird
Lark Bunting

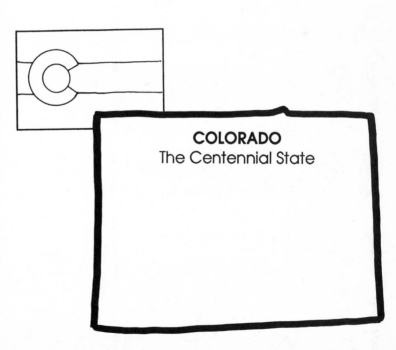

COLORADO
The Centennial State

Flower
Mountain Laurel

Bird
Robin

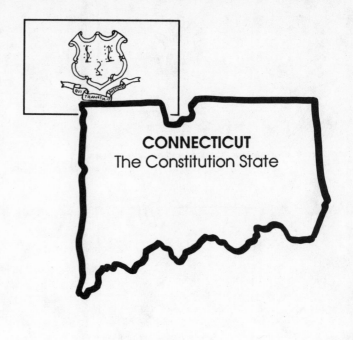

CONNECTICUT
The Constitution State

Flower
Peach Blossom

Bird
Blue Hen Chicken

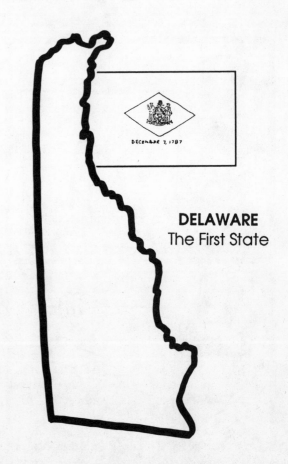

DELAWARE
The First State

United States
Florida, Georgia

Flower
Sabal Pine

Bird
Mockingbird

FLORIDA
The Sunshine State

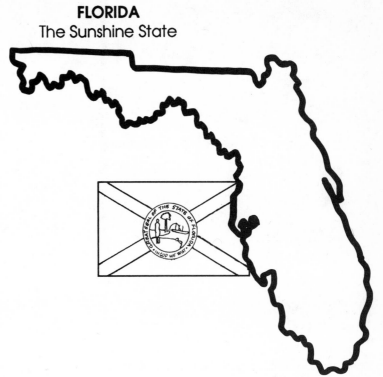

Flower
Cherokee Rose

Bird
Brown Thrasher

GEORGIA
The Peach State

United States
Hawaii, Idaho

Flower
Red Hibiscus

Bird
Nene
(Hawaiian Goose)

Flower
Syringa

Bird
Mountain Bluebird

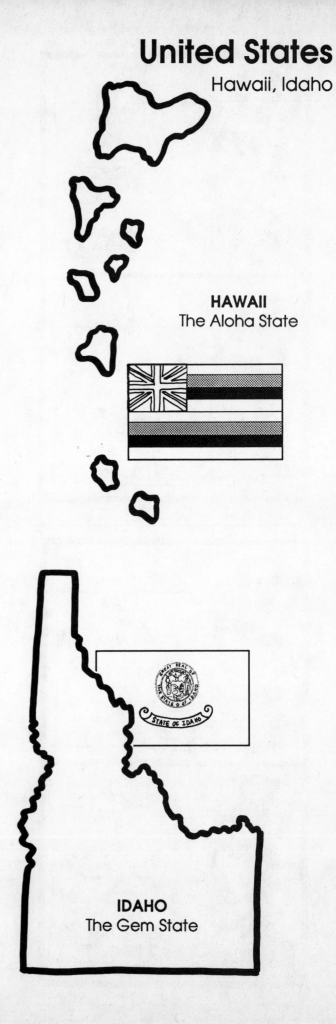

HAWAII
The Aloha State

IDAHO
The Gem State

ILLINOIS
The Prairie State

Flower
Violet

Bird
Cardinal

INDIANA
The Hoosier State

Flower
Peony

Bird
Cardinal

United States
Iowa, Kansas

Flower
Wild Rose

Bird
Eastern Goldfinch

IOWA
The Hawkeye State

Flower
Sunflower

Bird
Western Meadow Lark

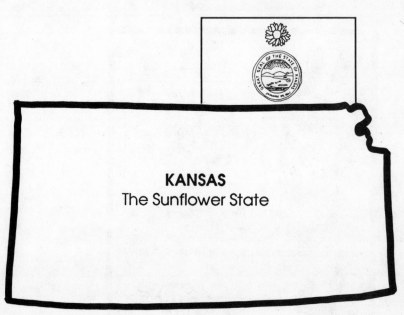

KANSAS
The Sunflower State

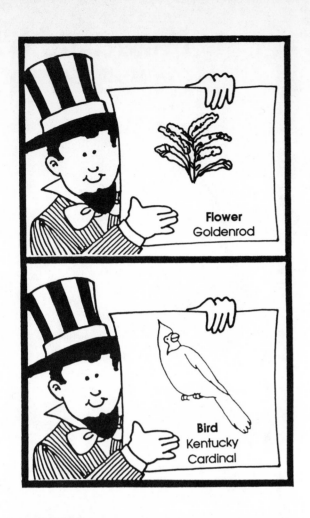

Flower
Goldenrod

Bird
Kentucky
Cardinal

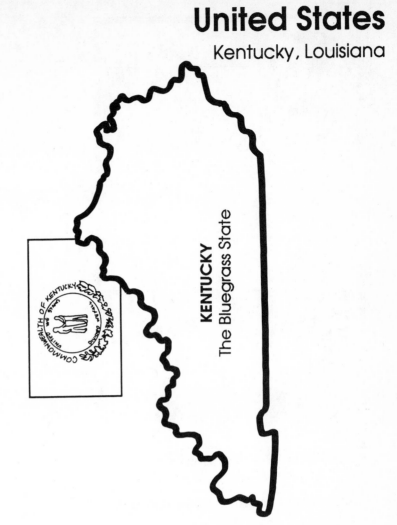

KENTUCKY
The Bluegrass State

Flower
Magnolia

Bird
Eastern Brown
Pelican

LOUISIANA
The Pelican State

UNION JUSTICE AND CONFIDENCE

Flower
White Pine Cone
and Tassel

Bird
Chickadee

Flower
Black-eyed Susan

Bird
Baltimore Oriole

MAINE
The Pine Tree State

MARYLAND
The Old Line State

Flower
Mayflower

Bird
Chickadee

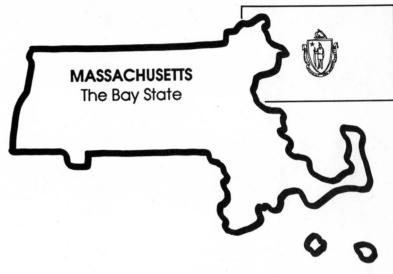

MASSACHUSETTS
The Bay State

Flower
Apple Blossom

Bird
Robin

MICHIGAN
The Great Lake State

Flower
Pink and White
Lady's-slipper

Bird
Goldfinch

Flower
Magnolia

Bird
Mockingbird

MINNESOTA
The Gopher State

MISSISSIPPI
The Magnolia State

Flower
Hawthorn

Bird
Bluebird

MISSOURI
The Show Me State

Flower
Bitterroot

Bird
Western Meadow
Lark

MONTANA
The Treasure State

Flower
Goldenrod

Bird
Western
Meadow Lark

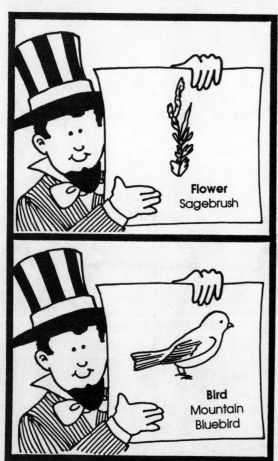

Flower
Sagebrush

Bird
Mountain
Bluebird

United States
Nebraska, Nevada

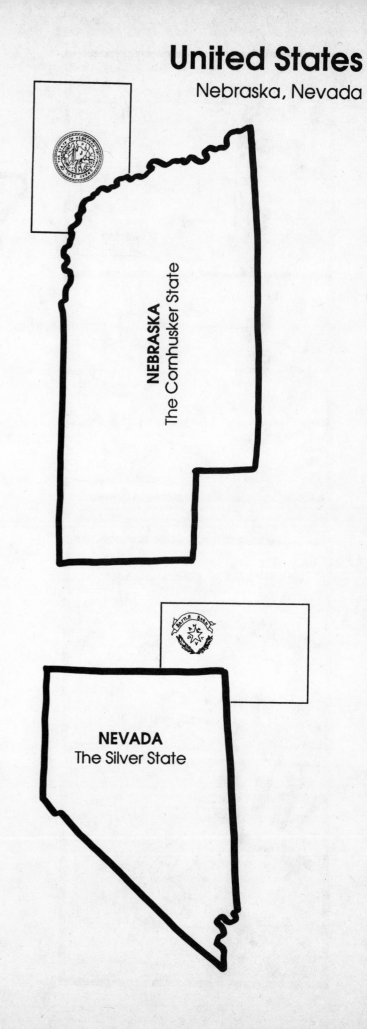

NEBRASKA
The Cornhusker State

NEVADA
The Silver State

United States
New Hampshire, New Jersey

Flower
Purple Lilac

Bird
Purple Finch

Flower
Violet

Bird
Eastern
Goldfinch

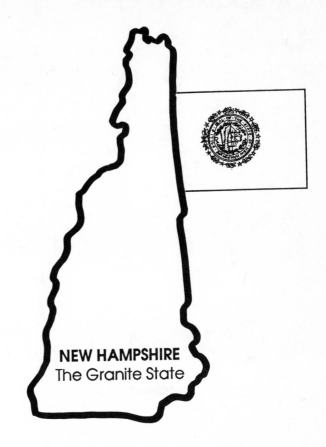

NEW HAMPSHIRE
The Granite State

NEW JERSEY
The Garden State

Flower
Yucca Flower

Bird
Road Runner

NEW MEXICO
The Land of Enchantment

Flower
Rose

Bird
Bluebird

NEW YORK
The Empire State

82

Flower
Dogwood

Bird
Cardinal

Flower
Wild Prairie Rose

Bird
Western
Meadow Lark

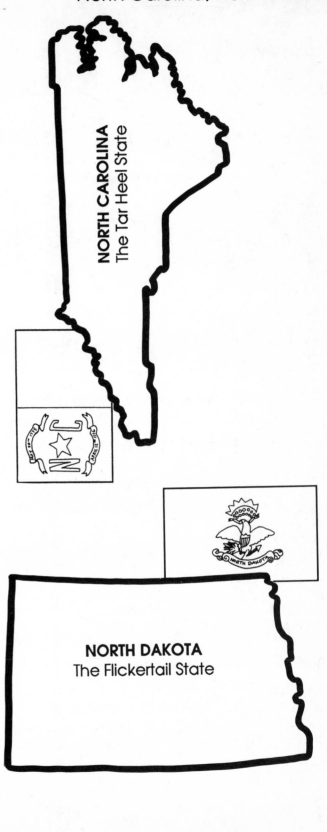

NORTH CAROLINA
The Tar Heel State

NORTH DAKOTA
The Flickertail State

Flower
Scarlet
Carnation

Bird
Cardinal

Flower
Mistletoe

Bird
Scissor-Tailed
Flycatcher

OHIO
The Buckeye State

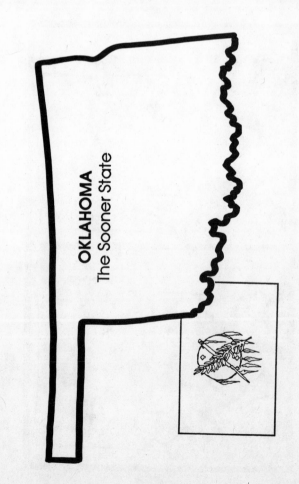

OKLAHOMA
The Sooner State

Flower
Oregon Grape

Bird
Western
Meadow Lark

OREGON
The Beaver State

Flower
Mountain Laurel

Bird
Ruffed Grouse

PENNSYLVANIA
The Keystone State

United States
Rhode Island, South Carolina

Flower
Violet

Bird
Rhode Island
Red

RHODE ISLAND
The Ocean State

Flower
Carolina
Jessamine

Bird
Carolina Wren

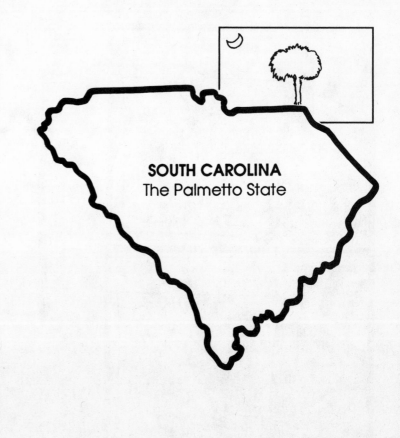

SOUTH CAROLINA
The Palmetto State

United States
South Dakota, Tennessee

Flower
Pasqueflower

Bird
Ring-Necked
Pheasant

Flower
Iris

Bird
Mockingbird

SOUTH DAKOTA
The Sunshine State

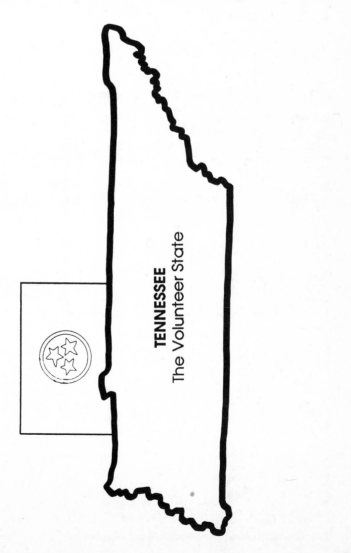

TENNESSEE
The Volunteer State

United States
Texas, Utah

Flower
Bluebonnet

Bird
Mockingbird

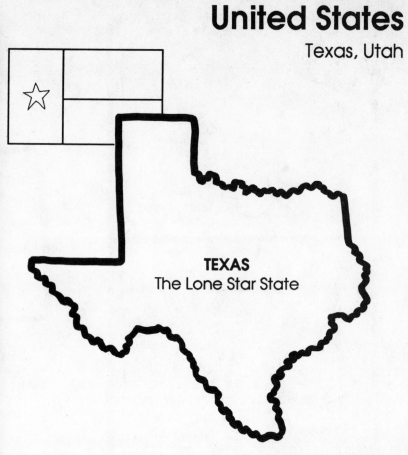

TEXAS
The Lone Star State

Flower
Sego Lily

Bird
California Gull

UTAH
The Beehive State

Flower
Red Clover

Bird
Hermit Thrush

Flower
Dogwood

Bird
Cardinal

VERMONT
The Green Mountain State

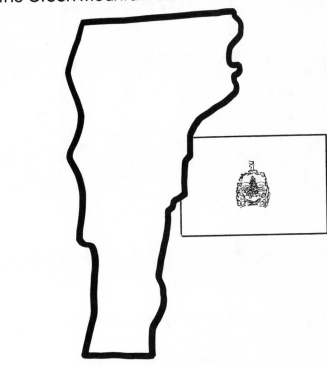

VIRGINIA
Old Dominion

United States
Washington, West Virginia

Flower
Coast Rhododendron

Bird
Willow Goldfinch

WASHINGTON
The Evergreen State

Flower
Rhododendron

Bird
Cardinal

WEST VIRGINIA
The Mountain State

90

Flower
Violet

Bird
Robin

Flower
Indian Paintbrush

Bird
Meadow Lark

WISCONSIN
The Badger State

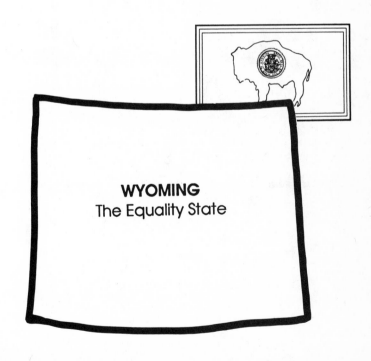

WYOMING
The Equality State

White House

Capitol Building

Lincoln Memorial

Washington Monument

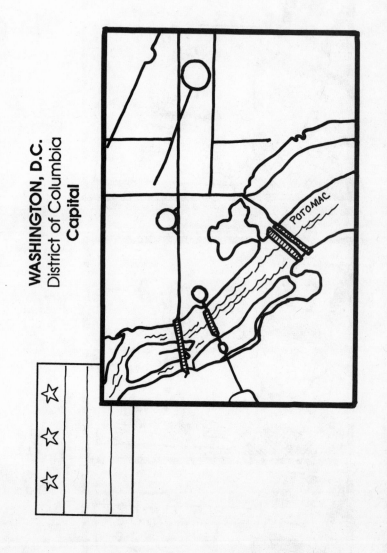

WASHINGTON, D.C.
District of Columbia
Capital

Canadian Provinces
Alberta, British Columbia

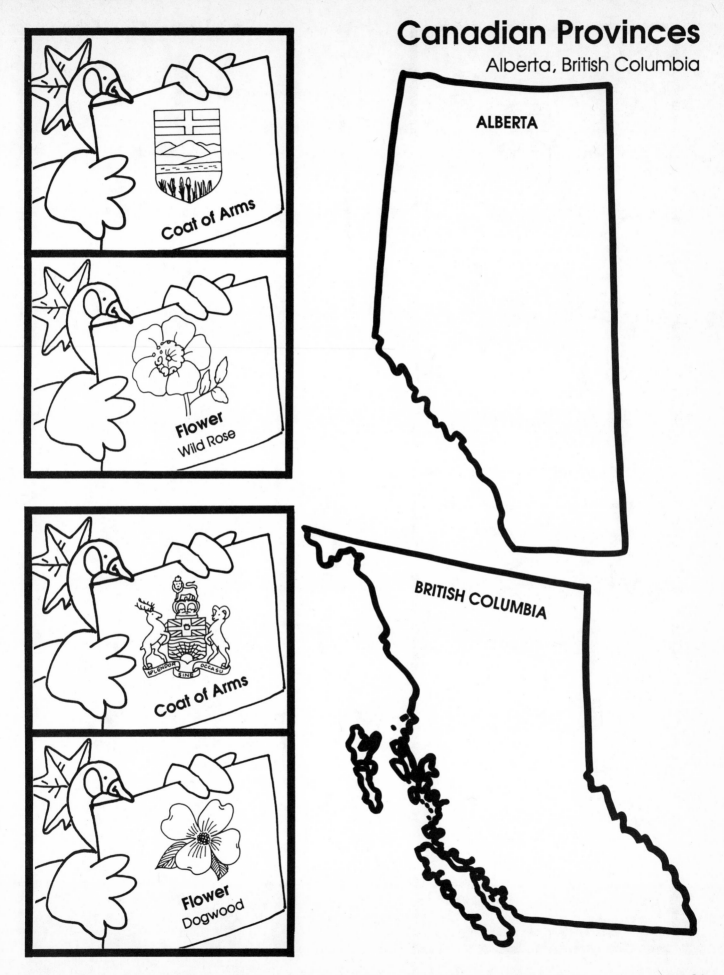

Coat of Arms

Flower
Wild Rose

Coat of Arms

Flower
Dogwood

ALBERTA

BRITISH COLUMBIA

Canadian Provinces
Manitoba, New Brunswick

Coat of Arms

Flower
Prairie Crocus

Coat of Arms

Flower
Purple Violet

MANITOBA

NEW BRUNSWICK

94

Canadian Provinces

Newfoundland, Nova Scotia

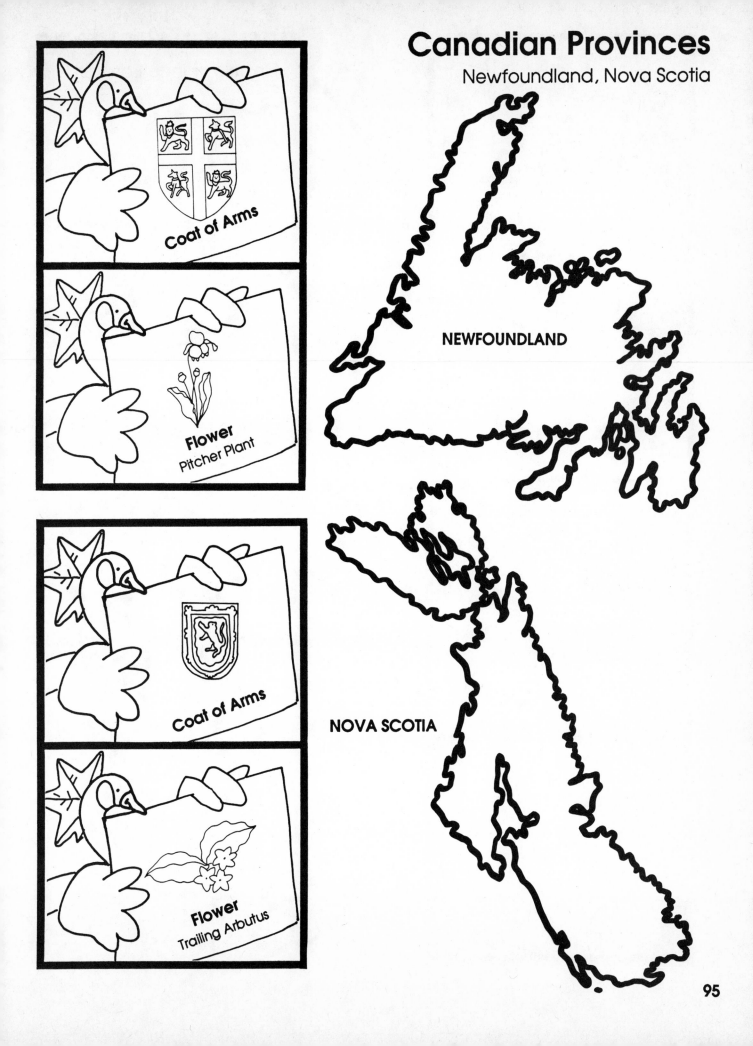

Coat of Arms

Flower
Pitcher Plant

Coat of Arms

Flower
Trailing Arbutus

NEWFOUNDLAND

NOVA SCOTIA

95

Coat of Arms

Flower
Trillium

Coat of Arms

Flower
Pink Lady's-slipper

Canadian Provinces
Ontario, Prince Edward Island

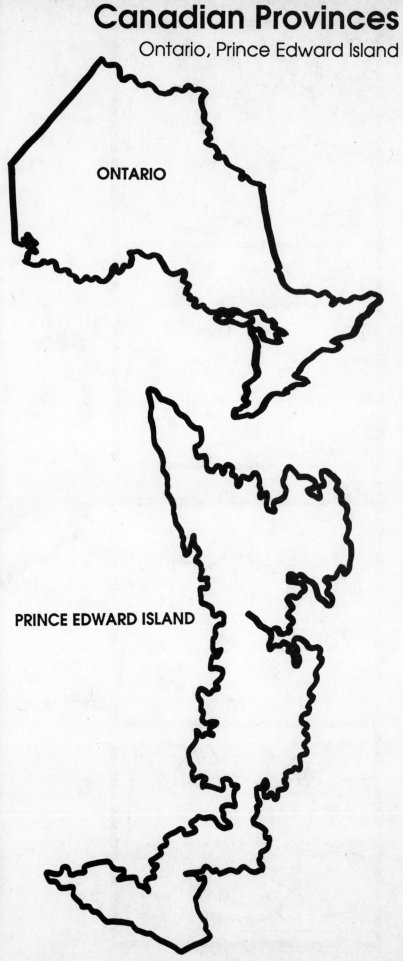

ONTARIO

PRINCE EDWARD ISLAND

Canadian Provinces
Quebec, Saskatchewan

Coat of Arms

Flower
Madonna Lily

Coat of Arms

Flower
Prairie Lily

QUEBEC

SASKATCHEWAN

Countries of Africa
Cameroun
Central African Republic
Chad
Congo
Republic of the Congo
Dahomey
Egypt
Ethiopia
Gabon
Ghana
Guinea
Ivory Coast
Liberia
Libya
Madagascar

Countries of Africa (cont'd)
Mali
Mauritania
Morocco
Niger
Nigeria
Senegal
Sierra Leone
Somali Republic
South Africa
Sudan
Tanganyika
Togo
Tunisia
Upper Volta

Countries of Asia

Aden
Aden Protect.
Afghanistan
Bahrain
Bhutan
Borneo
Brunei
Burma
Cambodia
Ceylon
China
Cyprus
Formosa (Taiwan)
Hong Kong
India
Indonesia
Iran (Persia)
Iraq
Israel
Japan
Jordan
Korea (North)
Korea (South)

Countries of Asia (cont'd)

Kuwait
Laos
Lebanon
Malaya
Mongolia (Outer)
Nepal
Oman
Pakistan
Philippines
Qatar
Russia (in Asia)
Sarawak
Saudi Arabia
Singapore
Syria (U. A. R.)
Thailand
Tibet
Trucial Coast
Turkey (in Asia)
Vietnam (North)
Vietnam (South)
Yemen

100

States & Mainland Territories of Australia
Australian Capital Territory
    (inc. Jervis Bay)
New South Wales
Northern Territory
Queensland
South Australia
Tasmania
Victoria
Western Australia

External Territories of Australia
Ashmore and
    Cartier Islands
Australian Antarctic Territory
Christmas Island
Cocos (Keeling) Islands
McDonald and Heard Islands
Nauru (Trust Territory)
Norfolk Island
Papua

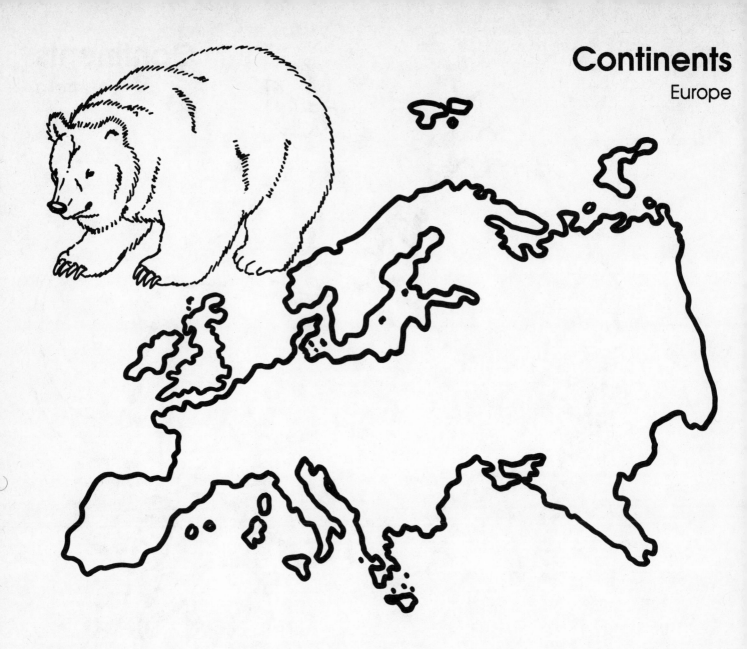

Countries of Europe

Albania
Andorra
Austria
Belgium
Bulgaria
Czechoslovakia
Denmark
Finland
France
Germany (East)
(West)
Great Britain (includes
England, Scotland, Wales,
Northern Ireland)
Greece
Hungary
Iceland
Ireland

Countries of Europe (cont'd)

Italy
Liechtenstein
Luxembourg
Monaco
Netherlands
Norway
Poland
Portugal
Romania
Russia (in Europe)
San Marino
Spain
Sweden
Switzerland
Turkey (in Europe)
Vatican City
Yugoslavia

Countries of North America
Bahamas
Bermuda
British Honduras
Canada
Costa Rica
Cuba
Dominican Republic
El Salvador
Greenland
Haiti
Honduras
Martinique

Countries of North America (cont'd)
Mexico
Netherlands Antilles
Nicaragua
Panama
Panama Canal Zone
Puerto Rico
Saint Pierre and Miquelon
United States
Virgin Islands
West Indies Federation

Countries of South America
Argentina
Bolivia
Brazil
British Guiana
Chile
Ecuador
French Guiana
Paraguay
Peru
Surinam (Dutch Guiana)
Uruguay
Venezuela

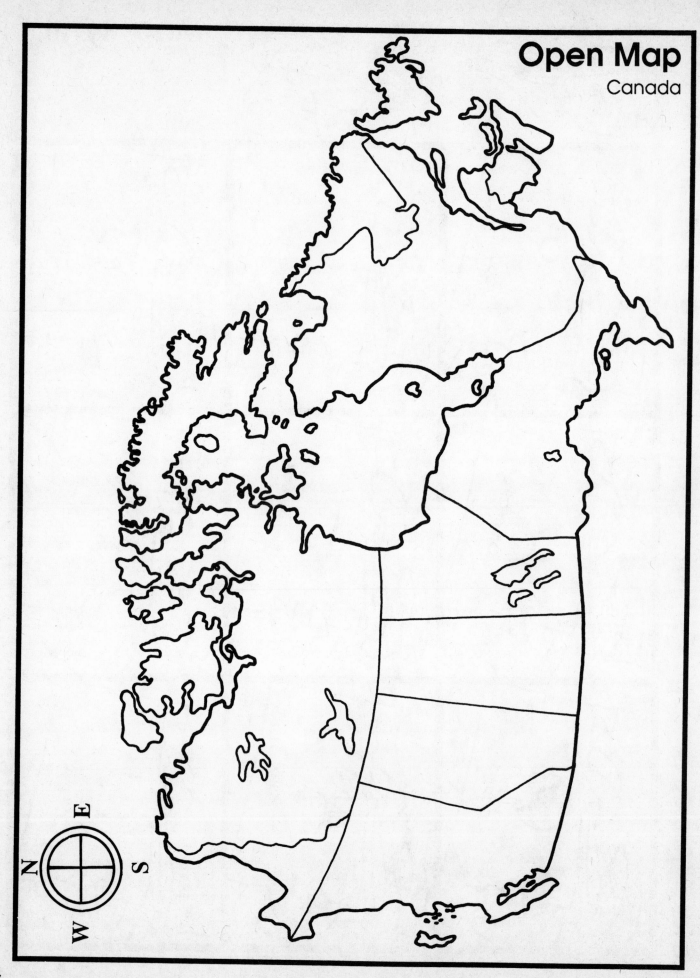

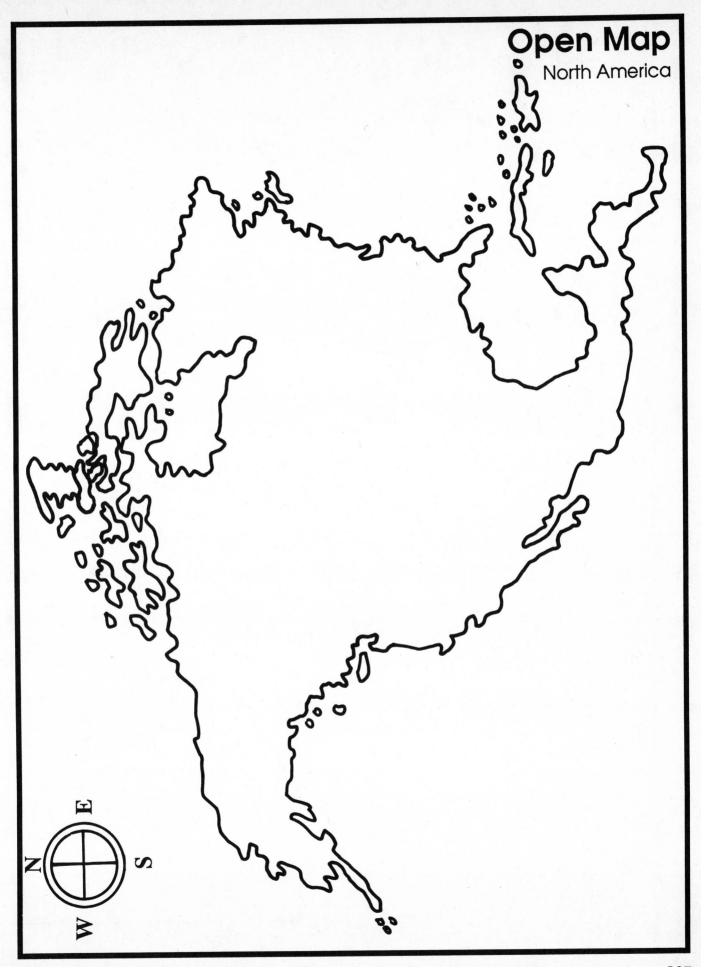

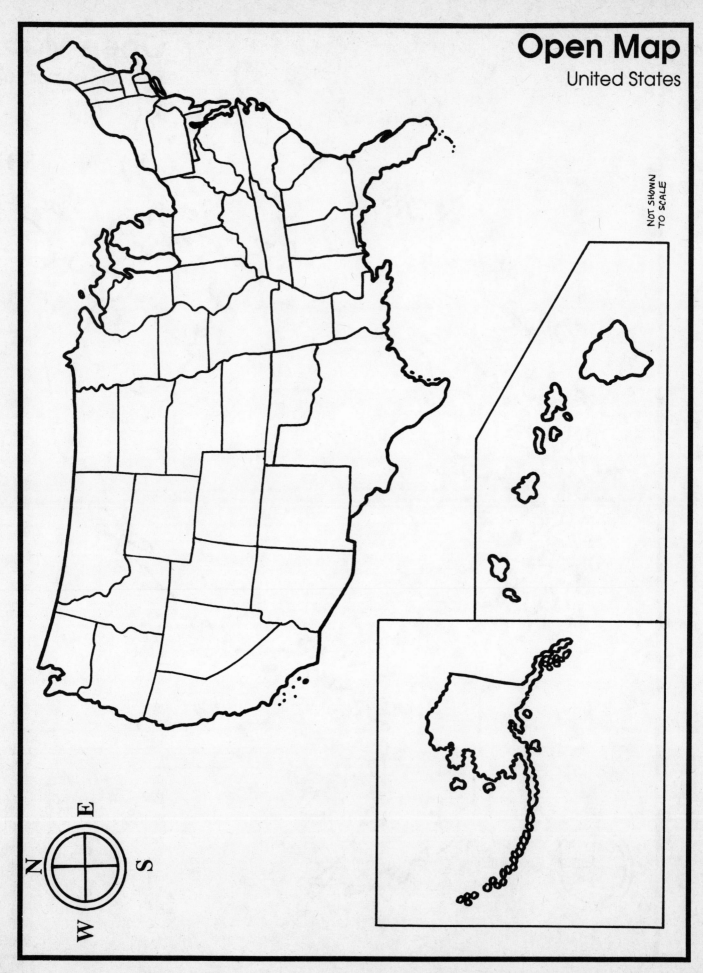

NOT SHOWN
TO SCALE

N
E
W
S

Ancient Wonders of the World

Statue of Zeus

The Colossus of Rhodes

The Pharos of Alexandria

The Temple of Diana

The Mausoleum of Halicarnassus

Pyramids of Giza

Hanging Gardens of Babylon

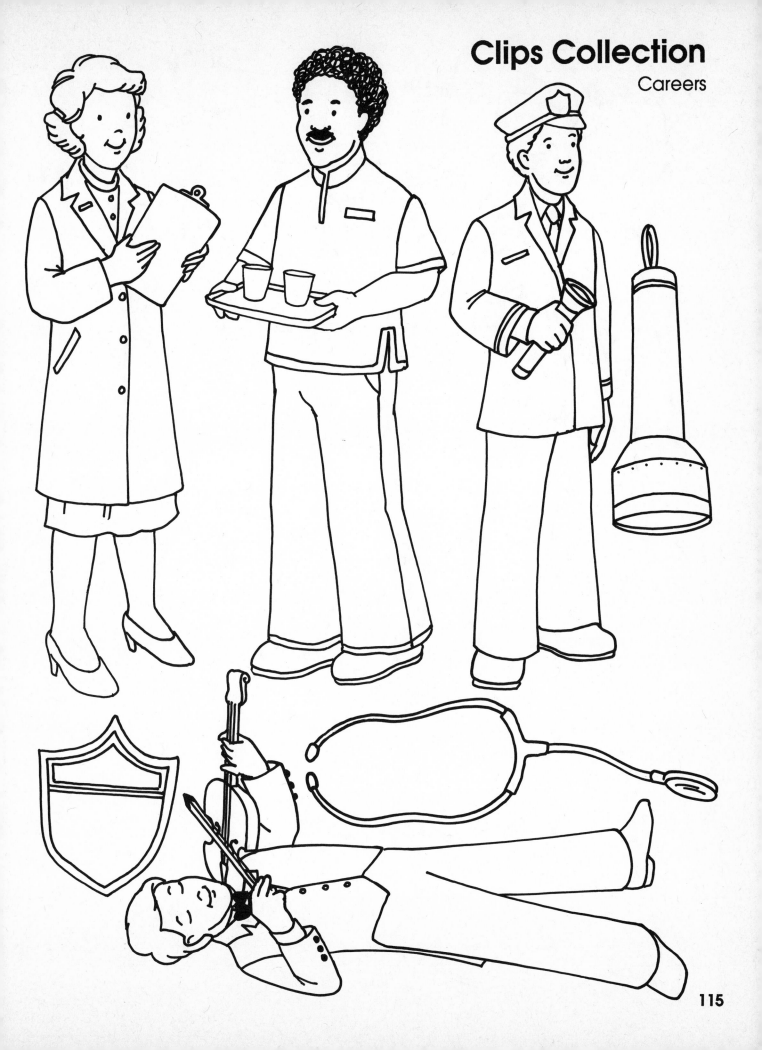

Clips Collection
Sports

117

Good Sport

Home Run Hitter!

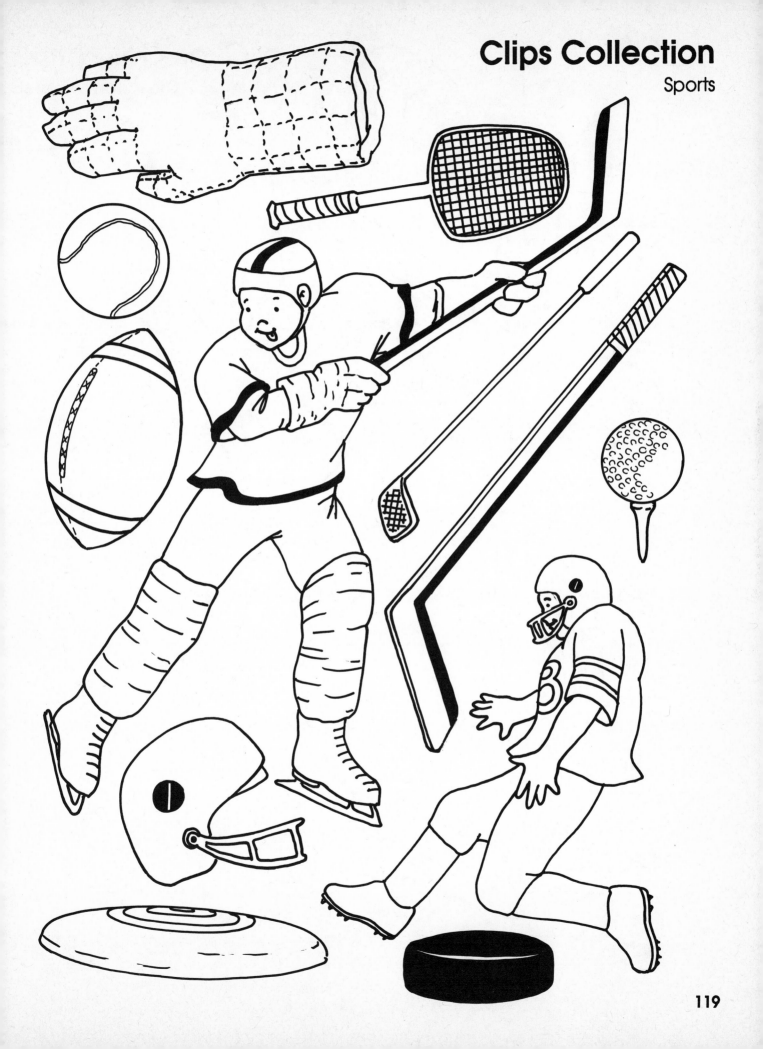

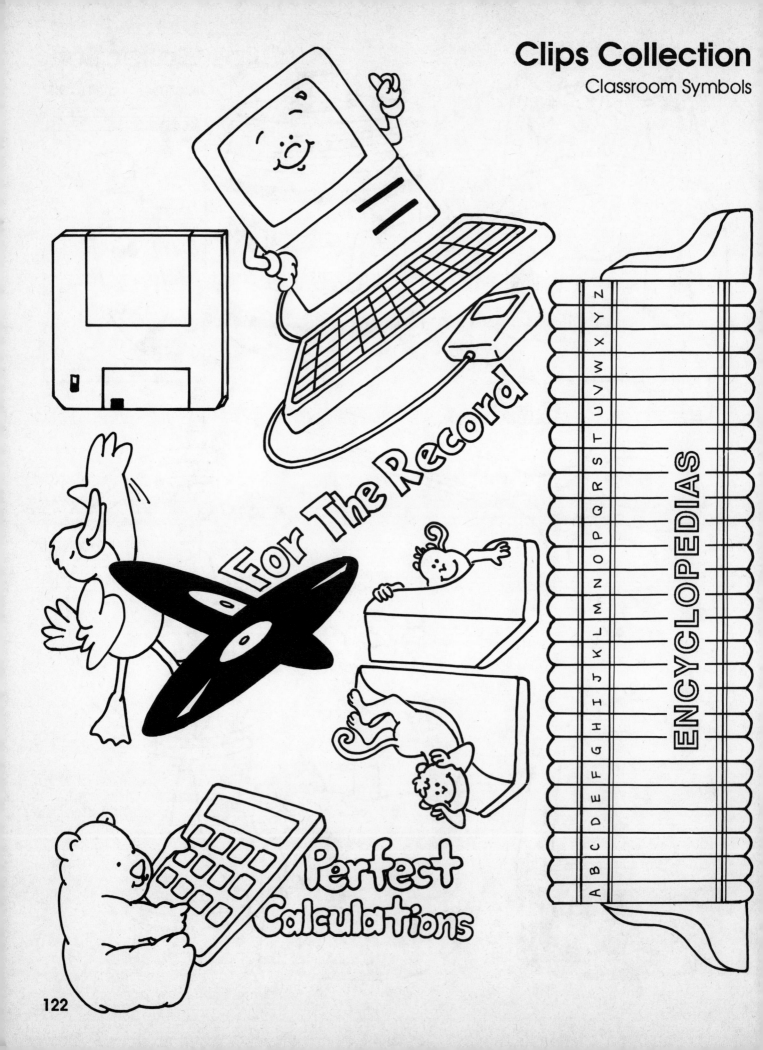

For The Record

ENCYCLOPEDIAS

A B C D E F G H I J K L M N O P Q R S T U V W X Y Z

Perfect Calculations

HONOR ROLL

Coming Soon

AMAZING ADVENTURES

BRIGHT IDEA • BRIGHT IDEA • BRIGHT IDEA

That's The Ticket!!

HOW OLD ARE YOU NOW?

Happy Birthday

HAPPY BIRTHDAY!

HAPPY BIRTHDAY

Popsicle stick

Cut out.

Cut out.

Cut out.

Cut out.

Popsicle Stick

Cut out.

Cut out.

Cut out.

Cut out.

Cut out.

Cut out.

Popsicle stick

Cut out.

Cut out.